THE SOUL VOYAGER

THE SOUL VOYAGER

MEERA JENKAL BHAT

LAUNCHPAD

An imprint of
Srishti Publishers & Distributors

Srishti Publishers & Distributors
A unit of AJR Publishing LLP
212A, Peacock Lane
Shahpur Jat, New Delhi—110 049

editorial@srishtipublishers.com

First Published by Launchpad,
an imprint of Srishti Publishers & Distributors, in 2024

10 9 8 7 6 5 4 3 2 1

Printed and bound in India.

I dedicate this book to

Higher powers for giving me the ideas and words.

My mother – Shanthi – for her patience and her immense belief in me.

My father – Dr. J.N. Bhat – for his resilience and strength.

My sister – Mamatha – for being my best friend & for always having my back in life.

Also, thanks to my friends for their countless help.

There is an age when one sleeps in peace,
It is when they are told bedtime stories.

Prologue

The young boy lay awake on his bed. He was an ordinary boy from a good home and family, but he had a curious mind. He had closed his eyes and tried to keep them shut, but sleep had known he was pretending. Now, at the darkest hour of another night, he felt the stirring of his troubled thoughts. At the turn of adulthood, he could feel the wonder of childhood leaving him. Science was explaining magic, the reality was catching up with dreams, and doubt was the clouding hope.

He gazed at the stars. Massive and luminous balls of plasma held together by gravity. He looked at the moon. Earth's only largest satellite and the fifth largest satellite in the solar system. He knew this was true, but he also wanted to think that maybe the moon was made of cheese or that stars were tiny shining diamonds.

"Was this what happened to all the children?" He wondered. Did they give up on the world of make-believe to become sensible and practical adults? Was there no way to keep the wonder alive?

He found no answer and became restless. The uncertainty of his intense thoughts was so dense that he was ignorant of a shimmering glow of light entering his room.

Until it said, "Dear boy, will you not look up?"

Startled, he lifted his gaze and saw a magnificent creature, unlike anything he had seen before. She was hovering at the level of an average human around the edge of his bed. She was made of luminous lava—her translucent wings encased in edges of brilliant gold. Around her was a sparkle of little golden lights. All this created an aura of auspiciousness. Her face was serene and soothing; like a pillow, one could rest their worn-out head on.

"Who are you?" He whispered.

"I am Fairytellus," she replied.

"Why are you here? What do you want from me?"

"I am here to help you fall asleep. Do you want to listen to some interesting stories?"

"What good will stories do?" He asked.

"The stories we hear become souvenirs of a world thought unreal. Each time one tells a story, one more part of that illusionary world becomes real."

"But I am too old for stories," said the boy.

Fairytellus gently replied, "No one is too old for stories. Stories are centuries old and to them, you are still young and always in need of reminders of the True Path."

And so Fairytellus began telling the young boy a story. One led to another. And to another. Before the log, the room was filled with echoes of the numerous stories narrated. Stories of great magic and mystery. Of creatures who flew and fought.

Of wondrous beings who had mastery over the universe. Of places unmarked on the map. The stories went on and on.

Slowly, the young boy's eyelids grew heavy, his mouth stretched in a smile, and he fell asleep. When he woke up, he had become *The Storyteller*.

Chapter One

The Old Man came down from the edge of the mountain and took a seat by the edge of the lake.

It was still and silent, as was he. There was a sound of serenity in the air. It was a sound of blissful silence where one could feel the pulse of their own soul. He took to a meditative pose and made himself comfortable. His body surrendered to the control of forces within and beyond. Thus, he waited there for thirteen days until the Young Woman came, to drown her tears in the lake.

The Young Woman's grief was so intense that she didn't notice the world around her until a single tear from the Old Man's eye startled the lake.

As the tear created a ripple towards the Young Woman, she asked, "Why do you weep, Old Man?"

"My tears are a result of your sadness. In a universe of interconnectedness, even a single tear of genuine sorrow is enough to create a ripple effect. Why do you weep?" The Old Man questioned.

Something about the calm curiosity of the Old Man stilled the sorrow within her and she replied, "Because the world, as I believed it to be, is lost. You see, I was a believer—of miracles, magic and make-believe. I feel like the materialistic world has robbed me of that gift. Of my inspiration. Now, I cry for the lost innocence and idealism of childhood."

"But you are an adult. Should you not be acting like a responsible one?"

"Responsibility, as this world has conditioned it, is a shackle to the soul. There is no freedom there. The race towards success is quite overcrowded. The world is clogged with such noise that one cannot even hear the voice of the conscience of their soul," replied the Young Woman.

"You'll do," said the Old Man with a satisfied smile.

"I'll do for what?" The Young Woman asked.

The Old Man did not answer her but instead, asked her, "What do you hear in the silence?"

"Nothing."

"It is best that you do so. From the trueness and blandness of nothing, emerges something. Perhaps you would like to sit with me awhile?"

"Perhaps I would. I feel like I know you."

"You know me in the same way the sun knows the moon. All loose ends are connected to a source. You know me, but you don't. But I have waited for you. And our old souls remember each other."

"Old souls?" She asked as she sat across from him in a lotus position.

"We are not the body nor the mind. We are but souls, who

are connected by cosmic charts, destined to meet or not meet as per our present choices."

"It is my present choice that confuses me. I feel lost and insignificant in the grand scheme of things. I do not know who I am or what I want to be," said the Young Woman.

"That is a good thing. It means you have begun to question. And when one asks the right questions, the answers will duly emerge."

"Who are you?" The Young Woman asked.

"I am nobody. I am nothing. I come from the Place of Sight. I have meditated in the mountains and seen the Divine Vision. But if you must know, I am actually a storyteller. I hear words, thoughts and ideas from the universe and spread the message," said the Old Man.

They sat in silence for a while.

The Old Man asked the Young Woman, "Have you ever asked yourself—God, where are you?"

The Young Woman replied, "I do. I ask myself all the time. I tell *Him* little things like before I finish this drink, give me a reason not to have another. Make me a believer—in goodness, hope, or faith. Just grant the beginning of a wish and I will wait for the rest. Give me a reason. A simple one. Oh! The games I play with God. Now the glass is swimming and I'm not yet done. Oh, the games God plays with me."

"That sounds very poetic," said the Old Man.

The Young Woman smiled for the first time and said, "It was part of a poem I once wrote. Poems which lie amongst other poems, in a deep, dank drawer that I have kept hidden from the world. I used to be interested—in my habits and hobbies. I used to be the best player in the world's playground. Now, I don't know if I am. I still like curious things. Oddities. Like a sudden rhythm of a song that arrests your soul. White cotton candy clouds float on a bright blue sky. The various shades of green, perfectly kept seashells, the smell of earth and rain. Little things like that move my soul.

"But the bigger things, I just seem to watch. Almost detached. Waiting for it to happen to me from a distance away. Paralyzed by pain. Frozen by fears. Shackled by stress. I don't quite know how my choices got me here, but they did. Here is: Uninspired; unhappy; and unoccupied at the moment. I live in silence and solitude. For a while now I have been. Keeping me company, though, are a million trains of thought, each running at different speeds on different tracks—screeching, screaming, sirens. And I am in the control room, overwhelmed by the numbers, unable to manage them; only anticipating with foreboding certainty the messy and massive havoc."

The Old Man said, "Adrift, you are in a world gone adrift."

The Young Woman replied, "Sometimes, in a moment, the many versions of you are in synchronicity. You recognize or remember a part of yourself long forgotten. You want to hold on to that moment. That feeling. You know it will pass too quickly. And you have to be strong to preserve it. I am at that moment now. I remember when I was a fifteen-year-old.

I can imagine the fifty-year-old I'll be. I feel a certain sense of security—knowing that things will be okay, no matter how difficult it may seem sometimes. Not all dreams can come true."

Once again, the Old Man whispered to himself, "You'll do."

Soft as his voice was, the Young Woman heard it and she said, "I'll do for what?"

The Old Man merely smiled and said, "Let's see if Time answers that."

"Who are you?" the beguiled Young Woman asked.

"For now, I will simply say that I am Syun. And what might your name be?"

"I am Taha," she replied.

They both shook each other's hands at the introduction and continued to sit quietly in their serene and silent companionship.

Chapter Two

Syun, who had gone deep within his mind, suddenly spoke, "Yes. Purity. That is in your name and identity. That is what I have been waiting for. Do you believe in auras?"

"Yes. The human energy field," replied Taha.

"Yours is quite bright for one so young. Still, I will tell you nine fables for the nine dark rings I can see in your aura. Perhaps these stories will bring you a sense of self—not only to expand your mind, but also to enlighten your soul. Do you wish to listen to them?" Syun asked.

Taha did not speak for a while. But then she asked, "What good will stories do?"

"The right stories, you see," replied Syun, "are pathways to different realms. They take us away from the ordinary and perhaps leave with us a touch of the extraordinary. If we choose to remember the morals hidden in them, that is."

Syun paused for a while and asked her, "Do you dream?"

"When I was younger, I used to have vivid dreams of places far away and I recognized them as places I have known. They used to brighten my night and uplift my mood. I used to think that there was an Angel of Sleep who would gift us dreams so we could wake up with hope. But right now, I think my Angel of Sleep, if she exists, does not quite visit me at night—for my dreams are scattered."

"Dreams are nothing more than stories that our subconscious combines with the astral world projections. We live in two realms—the physical world as we know it and the world of energy as we believe it. They both are real and when we sleep, they combine to create stories for us to exist in the physical world. Let me begin with a story about dreams."

Taha re-crossed her legs and listened attentively.

Chapter Three

Story 1: A Dream Parable

"Once upon a time, there lived a knight called Meir in the kingdom between earth and heaven—a kingdom across the skies called Etheria. He had dark, sharp features and a mighty tall bulk, but mostly he was a good man. Wrapped around his neck was a black cape gifted to him by the stars. It was made from the ashes of falling stars. As long as the cape was around his neck, he could find out every wish made by a human to a star. Despite his countenance, which was quite noticeable, he was recognized for the beautiful black horse he rode. Together, they could be seen racing with the clouds, feeling the gleeful wind on their faces, catching wishes that flew as a spark to the skies and settled as stardust on his cape.

"In Etheria, there was also a Forest of Enchantment, filled with many intriguing objects, deep in which stood the Tree of—"

"Wait, tell me more about the things in this forest," interrupted Taha.

"Oh. It has lots of charms. There is a tree that grows the roots of life; a merest piece of which is enough to give breath to a life taken too soon. In some parts of the forest lay the sands of time. The Gods take different grains of the sand along with juices from the root of life, they create the new-borns on Earth. The tree of immortality gives seeds that are eaten by the Gods to live forever. There are also the mushrooms of magic which are the cause for coincidences and miracles..."

"You speak like someone who has been there," said Taha.

"I may have—in dreams," Syun said with a mysterious smile. "Anyway, shall I continue my story?"

"Please do."

Deep within the Forest of Enchantment was the Tree of Dreams. She was lovely, with long graceful branches and a shiny head of glossy leaves. She bore the juiciest, silver-coloured fruits called dreams; each different in flavour and attribute. Each day at sunset, the knight rode into the forest to kneel at the Tree. Each day, she gave him the loveliest fruit—the happiest day, the purest love and many more. He always sat under the Tree, blissfully relishing the fruit, feeling the delight rush into every sinew of his being.

After his dream was tucked away into his being, he collected the scattered, fallen and broken dreams, and plucked the ripest of dreams to put them in a basket. Then he waited. From the hour of dusk passing into the night, he waited for the eleventh light of moonshine and the path it shone. He rode down this path towards Earth, where mankind lay asleep. It was not an easy journey, but he was used to it, for there were requests to be realised. Each wish is so unique that some need time, patience and resolution. And so, Meir studied his cape with a great deal of scrutiny and fed to each wish, a fruit of dreams chosen wisely. Some woke up inspired, some satisfied, and others simply happy—that was the power of dreams.

But Meir had a wish of his own. He desired to be the king of Etheria. He had worked towards proving himself by fulfilling his duties with dedication, and now his ambition was getting impatient. So, he went to the Tree of Dreams and asked her to give him the dream of fulfilment. This dream was not something that could be demanded, no matter how much a person thought they deserved it. It was a special fruit which blossomed only with time, courage and when there was an individual worthy of it. Hence, the Tree of Dreams told him to wait.

"In all this time, through all my duties, have I not become deserving of it?" Meir asked.

The Tree replied, "If you believe yourself worthy, in time your dreams will find you, as long as you don't give up or forget. You have now what you deserve and what does follow is not for you to judge."

Meir rode away, his heart heavy, his shoulders sagging with sadness. For how long was he to wait for something he clearly deserved? For how long was he supposed to hold on to a dream which seemed to have no surety of fulfilment? Though he heard the wisdom in her words, his disappointment was strong. What he didn't realise was that by getting impatient about the dream, he was losing it.

In the nights that followed, he watched the dreams of mere mortals being fulfilled. The more he watched, the angrier he grew. Slowly, the wondrous dreams he had eaten before began to fester within his fury. They twisted and turned, taking shapes, dark and gloomy. If only he had waited, if only he had believed—he could have stopped his dream of fulfilment from rotting. Despite all his strengths, he let disappointment overpower him, turning his ambition sinister.

One day, when he could wait no longer, his desire took on a grotesque form, he rode to the Forest of Enchantment. He did not kneel before the Tree of Dreams; instead, he shouted at her for his dream fulfilment.

The Tree shook her head sadly and said, "You have made your dream decay. The only way you can heal it is by starting again. Your dream grows on me unfinished, only you can make it whole."

The knight's face had darkened with uncontrollable wrath. "I shall wait no longer," he roared and took out his sword. He cried, "If my dreams will not come true, then I shall let no other have them." With that, he struck his sword deep in the heart of the Tree.

She shook in pain but tried to stop him from killing his dream. She whispered, "Knight Meir, don't. Knight Meir, please stop. Think of what you can gain with belief."

But Meir was beyond reason, and he plunged his sword

deeper into her heart. She writhed in pain and watched as his warped dreams took on a strength of their own. When she knew he would not stop, she took a long look at his face and said, “For every dream you try to burn, I will give them more to yearn.”

With that, she shattered into a million little pieces. Knight Meir tried to gather them all, but they soared beyond the skies and took the passage of moonshine, floating towards Earth.

Since that night, Knight Meir comes to Earth riding his black horse, trying to collect every little piece of the shattered Tree of Dreams. Every night, the little pieces of dreams look for a place to hide in the human minds. Since Knight Meir knows everyone’s true wishes, he attempts to turn them into a thing so grotesque that there will be no place for a dream.

It is said that if one chooses to dream more, then one can make more place for the little pieces of dreams to blossom and grow. And if one holds on to their piece of dream with all their strength and courage, then Knight Meir cannot enter their minds and steal away their precious dreams.

Chapter Four

Taha contemplated for a while and said, "Knight Meir, Knight Meir—sounds very similar to a nightmare."

Syun smiled and said, "Yes. You caught that one quick."

Taha replied, "Oh! So that's why we get nightmares."

Syun said, "Dreams often have higher meanings because they come from a higher place. Should we choose to interpret them, we will often find hidden messages from higher beings in them. But most of us dismiss dreams as something that just happens. Usually, good dreams are a sign that your life is on the right track and when nightmares occur, it means that your path may be mistaken."

Taha softly replied, "Then I think I have been mistaken for a while now. But it is hard to hold on to dreams sometimes when it feels like none of them is coming true."

"That is the true test of your dream. There is no guarantee that dreams ever come true, but the more you hold on to them and never give up, the more opportunity you are giving destiny to shape them for you."

Taha said, "This story gives me hope and reminds me of a poem I once wrote. Would you like to hear it?"

"Yes, of course."

D.R.E.A.M. S

I knocked on the dream's door. And asked for Her name.

She said it was all I believed. All I seek and what I want. Floating on a cloud of hope. In dreams, I am nothing.

Yet I can do anything. I can fly.

I can walk into Heaven. In dreams, I can dream.

Is it a sign of things to come? Is it a word of wisdom?

"Why do I dream?" I asked Her.

She said God has things to say,

For everything you wish and pray.

You may not believe Him.

But dreams you will.

The places I see are new.

The feelings I feel are strange.

Yet I know it from somewhere before. Is it a part of what I was?

Is it a part of what I will be? Does it all belong within? Inside of me.

I am hope.

I am the bearer of faith.

In dreams, I am the dream.

I smush the pillow.

And spread the sheets.

And look towards the starry sky. In the night's darkness,

I know a light will shine on me. I free my mind.

And close my eyes.

To see what dreams arise.

"Where did that girl go? The one who wrote that poem. She believed," said Syun.

"I think I let myself become too busy in the busyness of the world. When my dreams began to fail, I felt this anger at Fate and said that if everything is pre-written, why do I even have to try to believe."

"Indeed, Fate is beyond our choices, as it's written before we come down to Earth, but with sincere prayers—it can be rewritten," said Syun. "Let me tell you a story about the Tailor of Fate."

Chapter Five

Story 2: The Tailor of Fate

There was once a time when a wooden cabin was atop a cliff. For miles and miles around it, there was nothing but lush green grass and sturdy tall trees. Beneath the cliff rolled the waves of a gentle sea. It may as well have been a painting coloured by an artist's imagination, for no one on Earth knew of its existence. The cabin boasted no grandiosity. It was small and old, just like the man who lived there. The cabin was as old as the man had been for centuries. His legs neatly folded, his old face crinkled further in concentration, as his hands worked deftly with needles and threads. The man was a tailor, a *Tailor of Fate*. And from the moment wandering souls knew that they needed to return to Earth, they came to find him.

When souls left their bodies, they also left all their lives behind. They became without time, their past spent and the future unknown. They became without identity, who they were they shall never again be and who they are they do not know. The only thing they have in their possession is their Fate from the lives they had led. In a little black book were written measures of all the things they had done in their lives—good and bad, happy and sad, forgettable and unforgettable. Everything.

As the souls were welcomed to the other world, they were each given their little black book and were told:

"Read the stories of your lives. Understand and examine them. Then you shall know whether you were right or wrong. The more you realise the tidings of your life, the better choices you will make."

In fun and frolic, in laughter and music, the souls spent their time until it was time to return. Then they went to the only man in a cabin above the sea who could design their new Fates. The Tailor would study the little black book and draw measurements. But before he began to stitch together their suits of Fate, the Tailor would take the souls through a long corridor, up a spiralling stairway until they reached a door. He would then ask them three questions:

"Do you know your lessons from the previous life led?"

"Do you know what is to be done in this new life that you are being given?"

"Have you decided the choices you shall make?"

Only when the souls answered, "Yes" in certainty to all three questions, would the Tailor unlock the door and lead them inside.

The room was filled with rows and rows of threads of different colours, shapes and sizes. They lay spinning in their spools, seemingly ordinary. But ordinary they were not! The threads spun varieties of imagination, emotion, personality, ambition and more. With some measure of their Fate sealed, the souls could choose the threads of their new identity. The choices were plenty—artistic, scientific, creative, intelligent, idealistic, realistic, tall, short, white and black. Choices which would help to fulfil the purpose of their lives. Taking what they deserved and what they desired, the Tailor would then sew them for their bodies, minds and eventually their Fates.

So clean and beautiful was the Tailor's work that not a single stitch could be seen on the bodies he crafted. When all would be done, the Tailor would make a pair of wings and attach them to his design. So delicate and intricate these were, yet had the strength to break mortal binds and hence were called Freewill.

The thing with life was that circumstances arose unexpectedly. The collision of Fates required that an individual must make his own destiny. So, when the souls returned to their earthly new lives, there would be times when all hope seemed lost, when nothing worked out and everything seemed to be going wrong. It was then that they could use their wings as their only way to change Fate, as the wings of Freewill would fly them back to the Tailor. They could make one new choice and the Tailor would realign the stitches on them to create a new pattern of Fate.

And so, the souls waited in line to get their suits of Fate and wings of Freewill. After donning them, they would then walk to the edge of the cliff and dive into the sea waiting below—the sea of life. As they swam deeper into the sea, the waves turned and churned, binding the souls to their bodies. They swam deeper until they reached a thunderous waterfall that seemed to pour into an abyss. One plunge below and they were born as mankind. This ceremony went on for centuries.

Souls made their choices for new human life. They tried their best to fulfil the purpose unresolved, as it was in the little black book. They tried to be good despite bad circumstances so that their Fate would yield rewards. People loved, lost, cried and died, using Freewill only in the direst of situations where everything else seemed unfeasible.

In time, mankind began to grow sluggish. They forgot about the redemption of their past lives, the intention of Fate. They forgot that their actions played an important part in determining their Fate. They forgot that mistakes were merely lessons to point them in the right direction. They forgot about the liberation of their souls from this life and instead looked to satisfy their gluttonous needs for this life.

They thought, "If everything is pre-written by fate, then what point is there in trying?"

They said, "Why do I have to wait to become worthy of the things I wish to have now?"

They stopped trying to find enjoyment or pleasure and simply wanted to have it all—a bigger house that would make their neighbours envious, a better job with more money and a beautiful woman to adorn their side. Things that didn't matter, but they considered necessary. They began to misuse Free-will to acquire fortunes that they had not earned or deserved. No matter how insignificant their wish was, they flew back to the Tailor of Fate to have it fulfilled.

Now, the Tailor was not an angry man. But one day, when he saw the long line of dead duties and insatiable individuals, he flew into a rage. He screamed, "You people have abused the power I have given you. You deserve no Free-will for you don't know the right way to use it. You shall live your lives as fate determines, with no chance or choice."

With that, he drew out a giant pair of scissors to cut off every wing he had ever created. Two nights and three days it took to sever every last one. As the light of the third day's sun began to recede, it cast over millions and millions of scattered wings, as darkness engulfed the skies. In this blackest hour, people stumbled into the shadows of remorse and despair. The Free-will they had taken for granted had been taken away from them. Sometimes, the knowledge of having something does not make it precious, only the loss of it makes its worth known. And so, each of them lamented and regretted their actions.

The stillness of the night was broken by tiny footsteps. The Tailor looked up to see a little girl walking towards him. As she knelt by his side, he could see a shimmer of tears in her eyes. A single drop fell quietly. And the Tailor's heart that had been frozen with fury began to melt. When fury subsides into fatigue, all that is left is regret. It was then the little girl voiced a solemn request.

"Our offence lies in our foolishness, but does it require a penalty so dire? I ask you this—do not give me solutions, I shall resolve my problems on my own. Do not grant me ease, as I shall overcome my difficulties. Do not give me a map to destiny, so I can discover it myself. Give me instead the fairness that some turns of Fate shall be in my control, in my hands."

The Tailor looked at her young and determined face. At the youthfulness that would age quickly, in a prolonged lifetime, if he did not make amends. He saw countless faces bearing empty eyes and knew that he had no right to make humans prisoners of Fate. Life was not meant to be a sentence—it was to be a reverence.

He smiled at the little girl and stood to declare, "In your words lie the atonement for all our actions. So be it. I vowed to never make another pair of wings. It is a vow I cannot break. For each of you now, for all those who follow, I shall tailor beings out of what they truly deserve, but in every hand, I will leave stitches. The lines of fate in your palm are only reminders of what you can achieve, the rest lies within you."

Often, the Tailor of Fate takes a boat into the sea of life. He sits solemnly, dangling threads of hope, love, imagination, loss and despair for the humans living below. It's up to us to make a choice and take hold of the threads of our destiny. The threads we catch are sewn into our palms as Free-will of Fate.

Chapter Six

"What a beautiful story!" remarked Taha. "It's the first time I have heard that God does not control our fate, but we do."

"It is all in our hands, literally," said Syun. "Fate is nothing to fear but something to embrace. In the end, we all go to the same place. Heaven and hell are concepts that only exist on Earth. The inability to fulfil our potential on Earth is hell and the ability to fulfil it *is* heaven."

"Can we really alter our fate?" Taha asked.

"That's where God comes into the picture. With a mere click of his hand, he can conjure miracles, but only if we are sincere enough. That path to God is not complex. It lies often in being simple, happy, and courageous."

"You make it sound so easy."

"The simplest things are often easy, but we humans have a tendency to over-complicate matters. If you can just live a life of seeing the good in others, doing good, and being good, then Fate finds its way to God. What is the purpose of life, isn't that the bigger question? It should be. We are born on this Earth but don't belong here. We all belong to a higher heaven, but in this busyness of the world, we forget that our only purpose is to attain liberation."

"You mean *moksha* and *nirvana,* and all those concepts where we are free from the circle of birth and death."

"Yes."

"If everyone does manage to attain these, then there won't be any humans left on Earth. What then will happen to Earth?"

"Finding liberation is not something most people even believe in. We are so caught up in this material life that we often fail to even comprehend that there are other realms. Think of how selfish man is in thinking that he is the sole life form in this vast cosmos. There are so many entities who are eager to help us attain our final goal, but as we grow up in the race for success, we forget that they are mere trappings that prevent us from achieving our true purpose. So, Earth, my dear, will be filled with humans for a long time to come, even though our innate purpose is to find our higher selves."

"How do we believe in good fate when it seems like everything is against us?"

"Nothing is against us in reality. Suffering often occurs for a purpose. Think about gold—it is nothing of significance unless it is shaped into something. Shaping it into, let's say, a piece of jewellery means cutting it, putting it on fire, and more. From pain is born purpose. The stronger the foundation, the stronger the house. Hence, suffering disposes us of our weakness if we recognise it as an opportunity to improve ourselves."

"Those are mighty words, but often, in the face of a true struggle, one forgets to care about faith and belief," said Taha.

"Is that not the true test of character? God often knocks on our door, and it is up to us to open it," replied Syun.

"What if we do not even recognise this knock?" Taha asked.

"Then we must open the ears of our soul," said Syun.

"What is your definition of God?" Taha asked.

"To me, God is light and love."

"Light and love," repeated Taha.

"Yes, you see, light is a concept most people easily understand because we can experience it with our physical body. But God's love is something we often fail to understand because we do not always expect it. Yet, it is always there, like breath and air—a combination without which we cannot survive."

"What about human love?" Taha asked.

"Human love is nothing but a form of God and His love. That is why the point is to love all, even your enemies, as they teach you lessons, you might not learn otherwise. When it comes to the bond of love, it is said that we choose whom we want to spend our life in the afterlife but forget our choice when we come down to Earth. If most of us remember our partners as our own choices and our twin flames, then we would fight less and accept more," said Syun. "Do you want to hear a story about true love?"

"Sure," replied Taha.

"All right then. Prepare yourself for it—like all love stories, it is a bit winding yet wonderful."

Chapter Seven

Story 3: Bouden and Raeeni

There was once an artist named Bouden whose masterpieces bewildered the world with their brilliant beauty. People said, "The paintings of Bouden can revive a dead man." His paintings hung on the walls of illustrious museums. They sold at such high prices that he could have built a castle of money to reach the sky.

His fame was renowned across kingdoms, his wealth incomparable and so it was presumed he had no reason of discontent in his life. He revelled in the admiration for his creations, until one day, it didn't feel enough. He woke up that morning, it was like any other morning, but he felt something missing.

He looked around to see if anything had been stolen or misplaced. Everything was in its place, but the feeling persisted. The trouble of searching for something one does not know is lost, is that one would never realize its absence and it would be lost forever.

In the days that followed, Bouden tried to create his next masterpiece. He wanted this work to be so extraordinary that every stroke of the brush would etch his name in people's minds. However, the more he tried, the more he failed, and every stroke felt like he was digging deeper into the hole in his heart. His paintings looked incomplete, and as he stared at a fresh canvas, his mind turned blank.

This pursuit of perfection left him feeling restless and listless. The world, he felt, no longer provided him with a muse or an inspiration, and he knew that his work reflected it. Mediocrity, to him, was like a slow death. In the beginning, it makes one complacent about creativity, and when that feeling is settled, it makes one incapable of passion and creating to the best of their abilities.

It makes one stagnate in average creations, and the motivation to achieve greatness is lost until their spirit withered on ideas that are derivative and insipid. So, with every day that the world continued to applaud his artistic genius, Bouden's feeling of being a fraud increased. In his heart, he knew he was in danger of losing his originality.

The convoluted lines and strokes of his art may have been confused as admiration, but they could not hide the truth—complexity was a cover-up for the lack of a genuine idea, which simplicity would have exposed.

He could not remember the last time he had felt awed, moved, or excited by anything. At twenty-five, he was too young to feel such magnitudes of world-weariness. The trouble with living life, he decided, was that people unknowingly fall into patterns and routines, until the things that had once brought joy fail to evoke delight.

The habitual-ness of existence was hard to break. So, people continued doing the things they did, without making any efforts to do something appreciative or different—equivalent to the walking dead. Bouden thought, '*There is no point to my life if I can't paint.*'

Having now recognised the complexity of his problem, Bouden decided to renounce the world as he knew it and head out in search of new experiences that he hoped would make him feel alive again. Save for his art materials, he left everything else behind and was surprised to feel less burdened already. He realized that sometimes, the familiarity of a lifestyle could become a trap itself. Thus, on a dark yet twinkling night of the full moon, as the world slept, he started his new journey.

For months, he travelled to different destinations under different guises. He tried to find a purpose or someone who lived for a purpose. He soon realised that while the places had changed, the people had not. Wherever he went, people still were part of a perpetual race, to attain the never-ending or ever-changing wishes.

He realized that to live in such a world of competition and defeat, meant that one had to partake in this unavoidable race. There was no other option; the system and society did not let you have one. An individual could not have the strength to change or defy the system alone, so they too inevitably became 'one' among the 'everyone' that aimlessly followed it.

But Bouden was adamant about challenging the cycle of expectations and left the lush cities for isolated landscapes.

He lived off the earth's provisions—trees for food, rivers for water, and the ground for a bed. Gradually, he began to feel a tranquillity long forgotten, and the empty canvases he had carried along, began to be filled with sketches.

It was a re-discovery of drawing, started not with the selfish desire of a glorious outcome of appreciation, but only to relish the process. He realised that he had spent less attention on his art and more on the artist, seeking recognition and craving adulation for his work. In doing so, he had lost his purity and authenticity.

Why do poets write? To express emotions in well-worded verses. If their intent became publicity after publishing, then it would corrupt their gift. Why did artists draw? Since only they could capture the layered concepts of our world which eludes a layman's vision. Bouden had forsaken his flair for fame; he had forgotten that it was not he who would be eternal but his art.

Bouden lost sense of time, as he wandered around untouched locales, realizing that he—the world-famous artist—had discovered nothing of the world. He had been the frog in a very reputed well, but his perception had been limited to a well only. It was with these transformative thoughts that Bouden one day found himself on the banks of a river, attempting to portray serenity on paper.

Immersed in creation, he neither heard nor saw the streaks of thunder and lightning. Only when giant drops of water fell on his sheet, did he startle and dart for shelter under a thick-leafed tree.

He was resting under the rain when he first heard it—a voice. So enchantingly ethereal it was that seemed to belong to the heavenly angels. He knew it was a song of heartache, for it brought tears to his eyes and saddened his soul while still uplifting it. He found his feet heading in the direction of the sound, almost against his will. Quietly, so as not to interrupt, he walked closer and closer until he saw the person whose voice had captivated an unknown part of his heart.

Bouden beheld the sight before him and stood transfixed. He saw a beautiful woman dancing on the river. Her eyes sparkled like diamonds, her skin was an arrangement of shining crystals, and her hair cascaded like a waterfall. She wore a gown of silver and glass, the folds of which formed a part of the water, and her entire body was translucent water.

He had heard of sirens that rested in the seas, mesmerising sailors with their songs, but even as the idea entered his head, it was rejected. He knew she was not of this Earth. The ephemeral creature bent down, delicately plucked a lily to tuck in her ear and broke into a song. Her voice flowed like a gentle brook in a rapturous rhythm with the rain.

Somewhere in between her songs, as he stood watching the *sylph* spellbound, Bouden felt lost no longer, and the muse he had been missing was found. He was released. He was reborn. He was reawakened. He knew he would travel the world to be with her, forsake everything to have her, and surrender his soul for her presence in his life.

He chose a spot under a giant, shady tree and began to paint this vision. He used to observe her quietly constantly, afraid that a single sound of breath would break the spell. Soon, he was absorbed in his passion, sketching furiously and colouring with fervour until all his sheets were exhausted.

It was only then, he realised that it had stopped raining, and she was gone. A new feeling grew in him—a mixture of restlessness and regret. He knew that he had to speak to her, or he would never be the same. So, he waited by the riverbank, certain that she would appear again.

A week passed, as Bouden's mind turned between impatience and enthusiasm. He did not know if he was being foolish in his wait or smart in his choice. He did not care. He just knew that he wanted to see her again. Bouden was so focused in his silence that he felt the earth vibrate when the first drop of rain fell.

It made his feet tingle and his heart tremble. He began to walk slowly along the river. Before long, he was running furiously against the heavy winds, amidst the lashing rain, steered by a strange sense of direction. And then he saw her again—a fleeting glimpse in the corner of his eye that brought him to a sudden halt.

For a week, his mind was filled with the most interesting topics of conversation but when she came before his eyes, he was speechless. So, he did the first thing that came to his mind. Captivated, he stood in front of her; the world blurred and its motion slowed until he reached her. When he touched her, she whirled around, scattering water droplets to cascade upon them, and the world came to a standstill.

He was mesmerized as he stared at her radiant beauty, she too watched him with wonder, taking in his sharp features and soul-searching black eyes. In that movement, as time stood still around them, each heart was touched by a powerful and profound love.

Bouden fell to his knees, his head bent in the worship of the woman who had awakened him and said, "It has been believed that no description of love has truly defined love. It is knowledge that the heart knows without hesitation, the mind accepts without reason, and that the soul simply recognises."

"You are human. Are you not? It was you I sensed in doubt. You bring with you no danger. Tell me who you are, stranger."

Bouden replied, "I bow to you in the name of Bouden. Please tell me who you are and what your name is."

After a long moment, she whispered, "Raeeni. I belong to the world of spirits. My visit to Earth is a gift. I have known things beyond the moon and sun. Yet, I have never felt like this. In you, I see someone I truly recognise. But loving me may not be wise. You have yet to learn. From where I come, I must always return."

Taking her hand in his, Bouden made a proclamation, "I, Bouden, hereby solemnly vow, upon the realms below as above, upon my heart as yours. As long as I have breath. Evermore after death—I am yours. Sacrosanct in soul surrender. Ordained herewith to protect. To respect, to fulfil, your dreams, desires, and duties are mine. I bestow this promise. By truth, by time. Never to be forsaken, never to be broken. To give you the best of myself. My life, my loyalty, my love. Thus, this may be written and known."

His words resonated through the cosmos, and even though Raeeni smiled, she was speechless. The universe heard the ring of truth in his words and in answer to his ardent devotion, rained its enthusiasm. For seven days and seven nights, it poured, and they both lived in a world of their own creation.

They played like children, swapped stories of their lives, and forgot everything except each other's existence. On the eighth day, at dawn, as the dew drops merged with light rain drops, they both sensed their time together was ending.

Unable to bear the thought of their separation, Bouden said, "Why don't you come down and stay with me? I will love you until the end of time."

Raeeni replied, "Should I set my foot down on Earth to stay? After the raindrops go away. I will dissolve into the ground, having broken the bond by which I am bound here."

But Bouden was adamant in his hope. "I really feel that there must be a way for us to be together and belong together because Fate brought us together."

Raeeni looked long and deep into his eyes and said, “Love alone will not do. In making this dream come true. There is a way—though it’s trial-filled and tough. I do not know if anyone can love enough.”

“I made a vow, and I will live by it. Tell me the way, or I will find a way to be with you.”

“Seven are the things you must bring to me. To align the lines of your and my story. Each task will unfold when it is done. I pray with all my heart for your victory. Never think you are alone. My love will aid you with boundless magic. But only at the beginning though—for it is you who should pass the test.”

So, Raeeni blew a massive water bubble, which hovered mid-air. She also handed him a water jar. She told him to collect the seven items in the jar and that the bubble would be the vehicle that would inform him of and carry him to the beginning of every task. After one long final and loving look, she disappeared along with the rain.

Left alone, Bouden packed his art supplies and the water jug into a small satchel, which he harnessed to himself with ropes and gently climbed into the water bubble. As soon as he did so, the first task appeared as a water script.

Task One:

You must cross the seven seas.

To obtain a piece of blue sky dust. It is made of hope on the horizon. For things to be done and undone.

The moment Bouden finished reading his first task, the bubble began a fast flight. It hurtled past mountains, valleys, and villages until it dropped down in the middle of a vast, waveless, unknown ocean. As Bouden stepped out and waded into the warm waters, the bubble disappeared and he was alone. Bouden took only the water jug with him and began to swim in the towards the horizon.

He swam for a long time, but the horizon still seemed far away. Suddenly, the pattern of the calm ocean shifted and formed an enormous wave that came roaring towards him. With nowhere to turn but ahead, Bouden forged on, for he was a strong swimmer, and went under the powerful swell.

But it was no ordinary wave; it was the wave of despair, which thrashed his body and soul. It drove him to doubt whether he could achieve anything at all. Bouden braved the first three waves using all his strength, but the waves of despair grew higher and stronger, echoing woeful noise.

As the fourth wave thrashed upon him, tumbling him upside down, Bouden felt his body ache and his heart became heavy with fear. As much as he tried to keep swimming, the force of the current was too strong, throwing him further away from the horizon. The wave of voices grew stronger and taunted and mocked his capabilities until he felt a sense of hopelessness.

Drowning in deep despair, he felt disoriented and dazed, and the horizon of hope seemed unreachable. As the fifth wave hit him hard, he gave up almost all hope and simply struggled to stay alive. He felt himself drowning and stopped swimming because he felt there was no point in fighting a current this strong.

He felt the pain of this failure to his bones, in his inability to finish the first task, which had only begun, and the wave of despair grew stronger in his heart. As he was sinking, he heard a voice scream, "Bouden, believe!" It was one echo for a single resonating moment, and then it was lost in the thundering of the sixth wave.

But Raeeni's voice was enough to stir some strength in him, and he fought to reach the surface. As he did, he felt the wave assault him in the sea. He spiralled out of control, and a voice kept saying, *"You can't, you can't, you can't do this. Go back before the next of me kills you."*

Bouden's body was worn down but not his will, and so he struggled against the massive wave and resurfaced only to see the most gigantic of all waves heading towards him. It was large enough to strike terror into the core of anyone's heart, and Bouden felt a nausea of fear. Most men would have turned away and obeyed the waves of despair, but Bouden moved towards them using the remnants of his will.

Amidst the swirling noises and whispers, he thought to himself, *come what may, I will not give in. I will not give up.* That was his last thought before the seventh wave crashed into him and his world slipped into darkness.

"Greetings, strange one," said a voice.

Bouden heard it as a faint sound from miles away. He thought it was in his head and refused to reply, for his battered body and mind did not know where it was. He felt a splash of water on his face, and the greeting repeated itself once again. Slowly, Bouden opened his eyes and saw that he was afloat in the middle of nowhere in a now calm ocean. He looked around and saw no one. *Well,* he thought, *at least my head still works.*

But then he heard the voice again. "You made it through the waves of despair, I see. Most people sink into it." He felt another splash of water.

"Am I dead?" He asked aloud.

A laughing voice replied, "No. No. No one really dies in the waves of despair—they just do not cross them, either because of a lack of hope or courage. But you are one of the few that did, and that's why we are here."

"Who are *we*?" Bouden asked because he still saw no one. He looked skyward, thinking he was hearing angels.

"Look around you and the ocean on which you think you floating."

That is when Bouden realised he was being carried by a huge gelatinous substance. He stood up and noticed that seven miniature sea horses, with the central one being slightly larger than the others, were leading the stuff. Believing that the ocean had made him lose his mind, Bouden just stared, speechless.

The slightly larger sea horse turned its head and said, "Welcome to your hope carriage. Jerus, the jellyfish is your coach, and the seahorses led by me—Saran, the king of sea horses, are your ride."

Still astounded that such tiny creatures could pull someone the size of him, Bouden murmured, "But how is this possible?"

Saran replied, "It is a matter of mind over matter. Also, what science cannot explain, magic usually does. But only when one believes."

"Where are you taking me?"

"To the horizon. You won't be able to find it by just swimming to that illusionary line you see at the edge of the sea."

"Why are you helping me?"

"Raeeni told us of your tasks and asked if we could help where we could. Now understand that a lot of it, you will have to endure alone, but sometimes help will come in the least expected time."

"Beholden," Bouden said, "My manners seem to have lost me. I thank you, Oh Great King of Sea Horses, for making the time to come to my assistance."

"You are welcome. Let it be known that we love Raeeni and hope that your love for her will prove its course. Now, let's set a faster pace and reach your destination."

Hence, Saran commanded his second hand to swim faster to make their way across the seemingly infinite ocean. It took them three days and three nights, during which Bouden met dancing dolphins, talking turtles, and melodic mermaids, who wished him luck and told him jokingly to find them if he did not succeed.

Then he met the wise whale, who swam along with him for a while and told him that the piece of sky dust had many forms and that he just needed to be astute to find the piece to carry with him.

"No piece of the sky can be captured because it is nothing but air, but if you can see beyond what humans see, then you will gain a piece of luck," said the wise whale.

As the fourth morning arrived, Bouden found himself in a place that seemed like something out of a dream. The sky and sea seemed to mirror each other until one could not tell the difference. At the seeming centre of things was a colossal figure, half-man and half-fish. His body was more of an outline, comprising two horizontal halves, the upper half being the sky, and the lower half being the sea.

The sky held the cosmos, space, and vastness. The ocean held power and a variety of sea creatures. At his head was a blue cloud, above which there was an immense shining star. The figure was in meditation, with one palm facing skyward and the other below water, facing seaward.

Bouden was still soaking in the colossal creature when Saran whispered, "It is time for us to leave now, but best wishes, Bouden."

Bouden stepped off the jellyfish and realised that the water was surprisingly buoyant. He felt that he could walk on the water and took his steps closer to the horizon, all the while looking for what could be sky dust. He went about it silently so as not to disturb the great creature. Sometime later, he felt like someone's eyes were upon him. Bouden turned around to see that the mighty creature was staring at him. Not knowing what else to do, Bouden bowed to the creature and introduced himself briefly.

The creature bellowed, "You see me, do you? Only those who have hope in their hearts and belief in their beings can do so. It has been a long time since I have seen a human with such attributes."

Bouden told the creature, "I mean no offence by coming here, but I have a purpose to fulfil."

"Yes," bellowed the creature, "I have heard of your purpose, and it intrigues me. Do you really think you will succeed?"

Bouden replied, "I hope to."

"For those who have hope, there is a harbour here. I am Bekhi, one of seven siblings who guard the long line of the illusive horizon. We are guiding lights to those who are lost at sea, literally and metaphorically."

"So, it is the North Star above your head?"

"Yes, it is. It shines on collective human hope, but these days that hope is growing wearisome, hence, I must meditate to let it self-illuminate." After a pause, Bekhi continued, "Taste the water around you, will you?"

Bouden sipped on some water and found it extremely salty, beyond what an ocean should be.

"They are tears I shed every time a human loses hope and passes by me but cannot see me. The hope in the creatures of the sea keeps it in balance, but around me, the sea is salty in excess. It has indeed been ages since a hopeful mortal has seen and believed, because most often what they cannot explain or understand, they consider a delusion. While in reality, it is the delusion that lets them not see the truth. Do you promise to uphold the truth that I see in you, as it's a rare quality?"

Bouden solemnly swore that he would.

"Then tell me your story in your own words and cast some hope in my heart."

Bouden proceeded to tell Bekhi of his affluent life, its subsequent hopelessness, and how Raeeni had awakened hope in his life. He spoke of his love for her, which could not be explained in mere words but needed to be shown in action, for that is the nature of true love. He spoke of the seven things he must collect in order to realign their destinies, to find a way to be together forever. Bouden spoke earnestly and won Bekhi's heart.

At the end of his narration, Bekhi said, "You have made me believe in the power of your hope. As a gift, I will give you the first item you are looking for." Bekhi reached out to a blue cloud above his head and broke a chunk from it. He held the piece in between both palms and rendered it into a blue crystal and gave it to Bouden.

Bouden bowed and accepted the token with immense gratitude and asked, "What humans shall not give up—hope in themselves or in *you*?"

"Never give up because no matter what the circumstance would be, the choice is always within us."

"I will always remember that," said Bouden.

"Make sure to make others remember it too. Now, you have made your choice and must tread on it." Bekhi then lifted Bouden in his palm, bid him a warm farewell, and with a giant breath, blew him across the ocean, back to the shore.

* * *

Bouden found himself on the shore, where it all began once again. He saw the bubble waiting for him with the door open. As soon as he sat inside, the second task appeared.

Task Two:

Mid-way below the earth's core. You will find a dimension door.

From a clock that ticks hours rhyme. Take two threads of tomorrow's time.

The moment Bouden finished reading his second task, the bubble took a speedy flight to arrive atop a deserted mountain, with a cave on its peak. Bouden stepped out, expecting to find another creature, but was greeted with nothing but deserted silence. Hanging outside the cave entrance was a key bunch with millions of little keys in it.

Bouden pocketed it with the thought that if there was a door, it would need a key. He then wandered into the cave and saw a downward spiral staircase. After a few days of walking down the steps, Bouden's world was plunged into complete darkness. Time ceased to be of meaning and he did not know how many days or months he had been on this journey. Time transformed into the concept of a never-ending loop with no notion of dawn or dusk. But Bouden kept on walking and nursed his hope.

After many moons passed, one day, he came across a huge yellow-orange illuminated rectangle outline. At first, he did not know what it was, but then he realised it was the light emitting from a closed door. Bouden took out his key bunch and patiently started trying one key after another. For days and months, he sat there in the dingy cave.

One key after the other, one after the other, one after the other. All sense of sense stopped. His fingernails grew, as did his beard and hair. His body grew thin, and his eyes dulled with lack of light. Most humans would have given up and gone, but Bouden remembered his promise to Bekhi and Raeeni and kept trying until one day, he heard the lock click.

When he opened the dimension door, the scene rendered him speechless. Rotating on levitation and gravity was a huge hourglass below a small ceiling hole. The top half was filled with yellow-orange light rays while the second half was filled with ivory-silver light rays. He studied it for a few days to realise that the hourglass caught the rays of the setting sun and inverted as moonshine while the moonshine caught the rays of the rising sun to invert as daylight.

The outer cover of the hourglass was luminous and when he touched it, he realised that his hand went in and he could feel the threads of time. The purpose, he realised was to catch time before the rotation to a new day was completed. He then remembered a story from his childhood where the illusion of time was used to win a war.

This inspired him to attempt something similar. Bouden climbed up the side of the rock edifice until he reached the small crevice at the top of the hourglass. He used a canvas to cover the hole and then took out his art supplies. As night set in and the hourglass had moonshine on top, he balanced himself precariously on the edges and set out to create an illusionary rendition of daylight.

He painted without stopping, covering the entire ceiling with the sky, clouds and finally, the rising sun. His strokes were brilliant, and the scene was so lifelike, that anyone would have been fooled. As Bouden finished his final stroke at the time of pre-dawn, the hourglass stopped its rotation.

It was as if time had frozen, and Bouden hurried to the hourglass, which had paused just as the moonshine was inverting to the new sun's rays. He took out his water jar and was all set to catch the first rays of dawn before they hit the ground when he heard a lilting laughter. It was followed by a voice that said, "Did you really think time could be tricked?"

Bouden looked around and saw a woman in white, shaped like an hourglass. She was beautiful and had long, flowing hair. She had her hands folded and her head tilted in an amused expression.

"Who are you?" Bouden asked.

"Shouldn't I be the one asking you that, since you are the one trespassing?" The figure replied.

"You are right, but there was no one here to stop me. They call me Bouden. Pray tell me, who do I have the pleasure of meeting?"

"They call me Kala, the Keeper of Time. I have heard about you Bouden and your story. Tell me, did you really think what you did here would work?"

"I would do whatever it takes to make it work," replied Bouden. He pointed at the frozen hourglass and said, "But it looks like it did work."

"You think the power of your love and painting did that?" Kala paused and looked at him with slight mockery. "No, I did. I stopped time, and we are now suspended in between." Kala paused again and asked, "Don't you want to know why I did it?"

When Bouden didn't answer, she continued, "I was curious. I have been watching you for a while now. Do you know you have spent over a year in pursuit of these threads?"

Bouden was shocked into further silence.

"Yes," Kala said excitedly. "One year is not that much in the context of time, but it is a lot in human time. Do you think she will still love you after all this time, or even remember you? After all, there are promises we make and promises we so easily break. I should know, for I have seen it time and again."

Bouden did not say anything for a while, and Kala watched him silently. After some pondering, he said, "I cannot speak on her behalf but can only hope that her love for me still exists. Either way, it is I who made a promise that echoed through the universe, and so it shall be I who fulfils it, no matter what the consequence."

Kala's mockery vanished, and she looked at Bouden with a sincere smile and said, "Your words and your deeds have moved me. Whoever loves someone so much to do something so brave and unique, is worthy of something."

So, she took out a small golden key, unlocked the mid-portion of the hourglass took out two threads—one yellow and the other orange—and handed them to Bouden.

As she did so, she said, "Do you realise that the hourglass is shaped like the infinity sign? It symbolises time as a limitless loop—perfectly symmetrical and unending. She is an immortal, and you a mortal. One day, your time will cease and hers will not. For realms to merge, time needs to go beyond the conditions of this world's concept of time. As I give you these threads, I gift you *love's limitlessness*."

Bouden took the threads in reverence and put them in his water jar along with the blue crystal. Kala then clapped her hands, and the suspended hourglass began to rotate again, showing the rise of a new dawn.

With another clap, Kala restored Bouden's old form to him. With a soft smile, she said, "Go to her, Bouden, and God willing, your times will align."

Bouden bowed to Kala and said, “I do not have the words to thank you for your kindness.”

Kala replied, “I have seen your devotion, it’s not easy to cultivate during these times. Keep them as per my wishes to you.” Kala created a pathway portal. “Enter this, and it will lead you to the entrance of the cave.” Then she vanished as quietly as she had arrived.

Bouden entered the pathway portal and walked for a while before finding himself facing daylight. He soaked in the broad sun for one long moment and then saw the bubble appear before him. With a final mental thank you to Kala, Bouden stepped aboard his bubble vehicle.

* * *

As soon as he did so, the watery script began to display task three.

Task Three:

Deep within the forest lies.

A creature of ashes rises.

A flame of faith you must gather.

Before you can journey any further.

The moment Bouden finished reading his third task, the bubble began a flight, soaring above seas and scenes until it arrived at the edge of a forest. Taking his satchel with him, Bouden began a journey into the forest. He found that it was an enchanting forest with tall green trees and wondrous creatures of vast variety.

As he made his passage, little animals came out to see him, for they all knew Raeeni and loved her. Little by little, as their shyness dissipated, they told Bouden stories of how Raeeni had helped them time and time again, a product of her generous spirit. A little wolf also told of how Raeeni had healed his paw with water when he had been pricked by a thorn. All these stories made Bouden love her all the more. He felt he must try his best to reunite with her.

After some time, the elder owl finally took up the courage to ask if Bouden could do them all a favour. Generous in heart himself, Bouden agreed before even knowing what it was. The owl said that their king, the brave-hearted lion, had fallen into melancholy. Adventurous, he had explored every inch of the forest until he felt there was nothing left to excite him anymore.

The owl said that the lion was a good-hearted beast and had ruled them into peace and prosperity, but now in his melancholy, nothing interested him anymore, and they were all worried about their shared Fate. Bouden asked to take him to their king, and they did.

When Bouden appeared before the lion, he had just finished yet another mighty yawn. Upon seeing the human before him, the lion roared in a dull tone, "As you well know, I do not eat humans, but I just may eat this one out of sheer boredom."

Bouden said nothing but stared at the massive lion with sadness.

Upon his silence, the lion yawned again and said, "Fine,

run if you must, and I will chase you. But I do not think it will be much fun for you, as you are nothing but skin and bones."

Bouden said, "Oh, great king, I am not here to run, but if can, please sit still with your eyes closed for a while. I think I can be of some help to you."

The lion replied with just a hint of amusement, "Oh well. I have nothing else to do anyway, and you have interested me enough."

So, the lion king sat still for a while with his eyes closed. A few hours passed, and then Bouden told the lion to open his eyes. When the lion obeyed, he was amazed to see a real reflection of himself held up by Bouden.

"Why!" The lion cried. "I have never seen anything quite like that. Look at the way the light colours my face and look at the life you have put into my body. I must learn how you did that. Oh, I must!"

So, Bouden spent his days teaching and training the king of the forest to paint and sketch. They used leaves for canvases and created colours from fruits and flowers. The forest creatures were so thrilled to see the re-kindled enthusiasm in their king, and they worked together to create canvases and colours.

While the forest buzzed with activity, Bouden tolerantly trained his apprentice to draw, using the forest itself, as a muse. It was not an easy task, for the lion had stubby paws and little patience. He was easily distracted and needed a lot of praise from his teacher. Many months passed with little improvement, but Bouden kept faith in his student because he knew that art had healing powers and he wanted to witness the little forest filled with joy again.

Many more months passed, and the lion, who had had little enthusiasm for anything, finally developed his artistic style. His paintings could be seen hanging from trees, and his posture was once again filled with energy instead of the stoop he had adopted. One day, Bouden took the king to a river and told him to sketch a reflection of himself within a specific time period.

Eager to start and prove himself, the king set to work, with the entire forest watching in anticipation. To everyone's amazement and delight, the lion finished ahead of schedule. When Bouden saw the finished portrait, he knew his work here was done and told the king so. Amidst the cheering of the forest creatures, Bouden was honoured with a garland of flowers.

Filled with a rejuvenated intensity, the king told Bouden, "You have given me something I didn't know I had in me. As a token of my gratitude and for your faith in me, I would like to give you a gesture of gratitude in return."

The lion handed Bouden a leaf that looked like a map. "This map will lead you to the path of the Flame of Faith. None can easily find it, for it remains hidden, but I have trust in your intention and so I hope you will find it." Bouden thanked the king and said his farewell to all the forest creatures who were sad to see him go. But they knew he had stalled his journey out of kindness and wished him luck in his venture.

With his satchel in place again, Bouden headed out into the deeper forest, following the signs on the map. He walked for days until he reached a tree that seemed to stretch out into the sky. At its base was a huge hollow and from the map, Bouden knew this was the opening he was looking for.

He walked through the opening and, after a while, found himself at the beginning of a maze. He knew that the map no longer served his purpose because this maze was a test. He knew that the flame burned in the centre of this convoluted maze and kept walking, hoping that he was on the right path.

He left markers behind so he would know if he crossed the same path again. After a while, Bouden realised he was going in circles and was lost. It was a massive maze and even though he could hear the crackling of fire, every step he took seemed to be a wrong one.

For days, it went on like this, with Bouden thinking he had found the path, only to realise that he was still lost. His faith began to grow fragile as he felt there was no way to overcome this challenge. Tired and confused, Bouden decided to rest awhile. Soon, he was in deep sleep. In his dream, he heard a voice say, “See with your ears, not your eyes.”

He dreamt of himself and Raeeni in a new land, living and laughing together. Thinking Raeeni was next to him, Bouden awoke, only to find himself still stuck in the maze. He stood on his weak legs and dragged himself further, one step at a time. He did not know how much energy he had left but decided to focus on hearing the sound of the fire, instead of trying to find his own path.

Bouden concentrated all his will on the sense of sound and kept going in a certain direction. Little by little, he felt the sound of the fire growing closer. Eyes still closed, he headed towards it and finally, Bouden began to feel the warmth of the flames. Bouden kept his eyes closed until he stepped on a spark of cinder.

When he opened his eyes, he found that he had found the Flames of Faith. He tried to collect a few sparks in his jar, but no matter how hard he tried, he wasn't able to. Overwhelmed and overly tired, Bouden sat down in front of the great flame, put his head in his hands, and began to weep. The endurance he had maintained during the past tasks began to take its toll, and he wept in futility. His tears were of such volume that they began to form little rivers around the flame.

Bouden didn't notice but a part of the flame turned into ash when touched by his tears. After his tears subsided, Bouden decided that he was still determined and decided to circle the huge flame to see how he could collect a part of it. His body was weary, but his faith was somewhat revived, and so he began to walk around the giant flame.

On his first six circles, he tried everything but realised no one could go too near the flame for fear of being singed or burned. As he was completing the seventh circle, he noticed that a part of the flame had turned to ash. He decided to collect that at least.

The moment he picked up a little ash, he heard a huge flutter of wings like a thousand descending birds. Fearing he had trespassed on something sacred, Bouden stepped back, only to see a giant bird emerging from the flame. It had a huge crest of colourful feathers on its head and chest and a pair of magnificent, golden gleaming eyes.

Bouden watched, hypnotised as the bird grew in form, with flame rays sparking around it. A little scared by this magnificent form, Bouden stepped back until the bird boomed, "Be still, Bouden. Your faith has found me."

Hesitatingly, Bouden asked the creature, "Who are you?"

"I am the Phoenix of Faith. I am touched by the tears of truth that you have shed and your unwillingness to give up faith in yourself or your cause. Through the ages, people have walked the maze in search of my power—the ability to resurrect life. But you are one of the few who have tread this path in the name of love. People do not realise that power is addictive, but love is transformative."

"How do you know I came here for love?" Bouden asked.

"The word of your story has spread throughout Bouden, and all await to see if it will be finished. Love is more potent than any other power the world has witnessed, as it has the ability to transcend space and time. And it is your love that has made me appear."

"Then pray and tell me how to collect the Flame of Faith," requested Bouden.

"Faith cannot be found until it is given." The phoenix plucked a green flaming feather from near its heart and gave it to Bouden to put in the jar.

It then called out to the forest for a feast and let Bouden rest the night near the warm flames. The next morning, the phoenix flew Bouden back to the edge of the forest where he found the travel bubble awaiting him. Bidding a fond farewell to the phoenix, Bouden stepped on for his next task.

* * *

As he sat down in the bubble, the next task appeared in a watery script.

Task Four:

Across the land of solemn sand grains.

A creature's conviction you will have to gain.

Therefrom, collect the eyes of destiny.

Thereon, come back to me.

The moment Bouden finished reading his fourth task, the bubble began a fast flight, soaring across sunscapes and moonscapes, until it arrived in the middle of a desert. Taking his satchel with him, Bouden began a long walk across the scorching desert. He was surrounded by hot sand and hotter gusts.

But in the winds, he could feel change and direction, and he went along where they pushed him. He walked for days and nights. The days merged into nights and vice versa. As he walked, he saw mirages, wooing him with lush landscapes of wondrous women, luxurious foods and wines. He saw castles made of gold and silver. He saw the sparkle of diamonds and emeralds.

The mirages tried to entrance him with glorious visions of power, money, and fame. Hypnotic as they were, Bouden understood them for what they were—illusions to deter him from the true course of his destiny. As he looked closer, he saw those who had fallen for the mirage—half stuck and sunk in sinkholes, with their bodies slowly rotting in the merciless and scorching sun. Bouden thus walked on, going where the whispering wind guided him.

One day, the winds stayed still for a long time. Bouden continued to walk until he saw a gigantic cloud of dust collecting on the horizon. It spread across the sky, blotting out the sun and rushing towards him. With not an inch to hide in the barren desert, Bouden stood facing it. He felt the violent, oppressive windblown dust come upon him and carry him, as it swirled and churned.

He did not know how long he was airborne, but suddenly his tired, aching body was dropped to the ground. Covered in sand and parched from thirst, Bouden felt he did not have the strength to move ahead. There was no wind guiding him either, and he felt utterly alone and de-motivated.

The sun stole what remained of his strength, but Bouden kept repeating his long-promised goal. Again and again, as if his repetition would grant him some will or make itself known to a listening entity. But his tiredness overpowered him and he closed his eyes unconsciously, picturing Raeeni and dooming himself to die.

At first, he thought he was floating, surely on his way to some higher abode, for the ground beneath him seemed to be moving. Bouden slowly opened an eyelid and saw that the ground was indeed moving but that was because he was being carried by enormous ants.

"Please do not shake, sir," said a voice. "You are heavy already."

"What is going on?" Bouden asked in a weak voice, both alarmed and amazed.

"We are the Soldiers of Fortune, sir, and we have been ordered to bring you to the Dream Spinner. He did not think you worthy of dying."

Bouden's head reeled with questions, but he had no voice to ask them. As if hearing his thoughts, the same voice said, "Patience, sir, we will be there shortly." Too tired to talk, Bouden kept silent and still.

Soon, Bounden saw himself arrive at a scrumptious oasis. At its gates stood two scorpions sheathed in golden armour, clasping long spears. Bouden was taken past them to a flowing waterfall, which seemed to begin from nowhere and flow into a river. The ant army took him around the corner of the river, to a secluded spot and dropped him there.

"Drink, bathe, and rest, sir. We will have everything arranged for you," said the ant leader and marched away.

After hours and perhaps years in the sun, Bouden lapped up the cool water and gentle surroundings. Around him, he saw tall date palms and fruit-laden trees. He took in the tiny sand castles, which seemed to be home to an assortment of insects. The oasis seemed to be covered in a ceiling of sparkling stones.

When he finished, Bouden was greeted with a pair of fresh clothes, fruits for food, and a vessel of wine. He sat by the river and ate, wondering how it had all begun with a river and now wondering what was in store for him. He felt like it was all a dream, and for a moment, he panicked that he had fallen for the mirage and this was all in his head.

"No, Bouden," said a voice behind him. "This is as real and as old as time itself. Don't you feel yourself trusting it?"

Bouden turned around and saw a massive spider with three eyes standing behind him. One eye was violet and the other indigo, while the third was white and had fleeting images flashing through it.

"My heart trusts it as a place of safety, but after what I have seen, my eyes do not," said Bouden.

"It is because you did not fall for the mirages that your heart has led you here," replied the spider. "We remain hidden in plain view, for not all people can reach us because they do not know the path."

"But you brought me here, or I would not have found it," said Bouden.

"Yes," replied the spider, "it is not your destiny to die yet. But you were close because the desert is a formidable foe. I do not speak of physical death, but when hopes and dreams die, the mind becomes a desolate desert. That is where I found you, but because of your last thought, I saved you."

"Why?" Bouden asked.

The spider replied, "Because they call me Damroo, the Dream Spinner. Come, let me show you."

Damroo walked Bouden to a large castle of sand, which seemed to be floating in the air at a fixed place. A thousand steps of sand led up to the castle.

"Welcome to the kingdom of the Castle of Earth and Sky. Do you think you can climb it?"

Bouden knew his will had been tested in the desert, but he also knew he had enough will to go on this journey. He took the first step, and Damroo smiled encouragingly and followed him.

When they reached the top, Damroo said, "Welcome to my humble abode. You will have ample time to see it if you choose my offer. But first, there is something I must show you."

Bouden followed Damroo into a large sanatorium, which had many pillars standing in an equidistant circle. One pillar stood at the head of it all and had the insignia of the all-seeing eye. Facing each pillar were silent spiders, weaving webs in golden threads. As they wove, engravings appeared and disappeared on the pillar surface. The spiders looked at the engravings and continued to weave.

Taking in Bouden's astonished look, Damroo said, "There are ten thousand and one pillars here, mine being the one at the head. I watch a section of humans with my mind's eye and send it to the pillars for choices and consequences to be woven. This is the room where destinies are spun, based on the choices humans make in their lives. Although the finality of their destiny is always the same, each choice results in a different path and must be woven accordingly."

"Are you saying we are the makers of our own destiny? That it is not pre-determined?"

"To some extent—everyone's destiny is pre-determined based on the actions of one's past life. But what one chooses to do in this life can alter the course of one's destiny."

When Bouden remained silent, Damroo continued, "You were meant to be a world-famous painter but one encounter with fate and one choice changed the course of your destiny."

"So, you know why I am here?"

"Yes. I have watched you as I have watched countless others. But yours is one of the stories that fascinates me because the course is still in the process. I cannot weave it—only you can."

"Does this mean I get to design my destiny?"

"One always designs their destiny. But what you have been given is a chance to alter it completely. You were destined to be a great painter, and you took every step to be one. Then you were destined to stop to seek something new. You were also destined to meet and fall in love with Raeeni. But the choice of forever was yours alone to make, and the steps you have taken since then were only yours to walk. So, the question is—do you dare to design a destiny?"

Boldly, Bouden replied, "I do."

"Then spin a dream worthy of its return," said Damroo.

"But I do not know how to spin a dream," said Bouden.

"Then learn," replied the Damroo.

Bouden thus stayed in the Castle of Earth and Sky, learning to weave with the student spiders. He learned how to decipher the engravings and weave people's destinies for them. It was a delicate job that required immense skill and a sense of destiny, which he realised kept changing as per the course of people's lives.

He noticed that the spiders were able to multitask, weaving many webs of destiny at the same time. But he could only do one at a time. He saw how a kind choice by a poor man led him to many riches. He saw how the generous spirit of a rich man led him to heaven. He saw how a stingy soul who got everything in one life, got nothing in the next.

He saw how love often changed the course of one's destiny, reaffirming his faith that love made the world go round. He saw how patience in a pious man paid off in prayer. He saw how those who did it knowingly, would get the bounty of it when they least expected it. Hence, he learned and wove endlessly until one day, he was called by Damroo to the head of the pillar.

"Thus far," said Damroo, "you have woven for others, and now you are skilled enough to weave a destiny for yourself. But it will not be easy, because I can no longer protect you from darkness, distraction, and despair, which are elements that try to forestall true destiny. There is no shield except determination to continue and discrimination to choose between illusion and vision.

"You and you alone will have to discern which cards would aptly play out your destiny and weave them accordingly. Should you design a destiny worth accepting, then you will obtain whatever you seek. Now, go on and weave."

Seeing as he had woven many a destiny in this course of time, Bouden decided that it would not be as difficult as Damroo had said and set to work in his allotted room. At first, he found it easy to keep pace with the parchments but soon, he found his mind wandering to daydreams of what could be and should be.

Hours would go by in his amiable fiction, and the web would not be woven by the end of the day. He felt pulled into his reveries, which were easier to envision than the effort of watching visions and weaving. He wondered why he even had to do it, because if thoughts shaped realities, then his thoughts alone should be enough.

Days went by without the web being woven, and Bouden began to feel a sense of desolation. He could not concentrate enough to finish the task, and the big dream seemed to be going further away. He began to misread the visions and weave webs, which were not accepted by Damroo.

The more he got rejected, the worse he felt, until anger replaced his ambition. He felt rage that a righteous soul like him was being tested and decided to weave anything he dared to dream of—being rich and famous, being married to Raeeni, ruling the earth and sky. Thus, he wove webs without following the instructions on the parchment, and they came out haphazard and fruitless.

Again, they were not accepted by Damroo. In the months that passed, he felt his fervour grow futile, and he felt like a failure. So, he just stopped believing and weaving. For a long time, he just stopped, engulfed in the darkness of mind that allowed him to neither grasp the visions nor gather his thoughts. He slept a lot and tried to dream, but they too, came in scattered fragments.

One early morning, Bouden dreamed, as he heard Raeeni call out to him to wake up from this abysmal abyss and finish what he had started. So real was the call that he woke up, thinking Raeeni was next to him. Even though he found himself alone, he could feel the lingering presence of his love.

For the first time in a long while, he sat before the threads and began to weave, trying to follow the destiny directives. That was when he saw the card of death before him. His mind, which had been weakened, was frightened at this prospect, and he decided to sidestep it as an illusion. He sat the whole day and finished weaving a web where he and Raeeni would be united.

He presented it to Damroo, certain that this time it would be accepted. But Damroo merely shook his head in disapproval.

Frustrated, Bouden screamed, "What is it you want? What is it?"

"The truth of your being," replied Damroo calmly.

The composure of Damroo's manner and speech settled over Bouden, and he realised that he had spent much time in pointless pessimism. He also realised that while thoughts were vital, the actions that made them work, were the main substance with which destinies were made of. The thing that was required when one weaved their own destiny was deliberate deliberation.

So, he began to read the parchments with precision, training his mind to dodge diversions and filling his soul with love's labour. It took him a few efforts, but after a while, he was weaving a web of wonder. One day, he once again saw the card of death, but this time, he saw it for the true vision it was.

He did not understand what death meant exactly, for it was not spelt out in the parchments. Death was a duality. It could either mean his physical death or the death of life as he knew it. Deciding to accept either, for he had promised to give Raeeni his love, loyalty, and life if need be—he wove death into his destiny.

When he did that, he felt a sense that his web was complete. He set forth to Damroo and presented the web with a new sheen of serenity, ready to weave as many webs as it would require if this attempt also failed.

Damroo took one long look at Bouden's woven destiny and then smiled and said, "Yes. I accept it."

Bouden did not know whether to feel relief or regret, for this was not entirely the destiny he had dreamt of. Damroo smiled and hung the web of Destiny on his wall. At that exact moment, the entire castle and all the creatures in it transformed into Divine Beings of Light.

The Dream Spinner then closed his three eyes and transferred their rays into a stone, embodying Bouden's dreams with His blessings, to create a jewel that sparkled in sheens of violet and indigo. Damroo, who was now a celestial creature, turned to Bouden and said, "Everything is not what it seems. Remember that. May the eyes of destiny lead you where you desire to be."

Bouden accepted the great gift with reverence. As soon as he put them in the jar, he was surprised to see that Damroo's eyes had grown back. As if in reply to Bouden's thought, Damroo said, "Some things are greater than what we think they are."

As Bouden stood with his head bowed, the celestial beings gathered above and blessed him to win in his journey of love and light. Although Bouden was reluctant to leave, he felt a new sense of strength seeping into him. So, he departed the castle which was now a shiny new kingdom.

As he was walking along the desert, he suddenly saw the water bubble hover over his head. He stepped into it to take a fast flight. He travelled for some time without any new tasks appearing. As Bouden wondered what was going on, he found himself watching familiar places. He realised that the bubble was taking him back to the river where he first met Raeeni.

* * *

When he arrived at the river, the bubble stopped, and he stepped down to the riverside. Suddenly, the sky took on a golden hue, and Raeeni and many celestial spirits appeared in the sky.

Raeeni spoke, "The corners of the world you have braved and sought. Have you the courage to finish what you've fought for? A passage may unite the skies and earth. Do you love me enough to bleed from your heart?"

When those words were spoken, Bouden saw that a golden dagger had appeared next to him. Of all the tasks, Bouden understood, that this was the true test of his will. It demanded honesty from his heart. He took one moment to contemplate the finality of this choice in his life.

Then, without a word of protest or pause, Bouden held up the jar of his task's returns; the violet and indigo eyes of destiny, the blue crystal of sky dust, the green flame of faith, and the yellow and orange threads of tomorrow's time. He then plunged the dagger into his heart, allowing it to drip blood into the jar.

The moment he did so, all the objects in the jar miraculously merged and burst into a kaleidoscope of colours, which took on their form of life and pushed Bouden towards the sky, creating a perfect semi-circle arc from the place where he stood under the part of the sky where he reached Raeeni.

Raeeni took Bouden in her arms and said, "There have been moments when you have stolen my heart, then moments when you have won my heart. But all the while, this heart was never really mine, but only yours to own. Thus, every time a true sacrifice has been made in the name of love, we shall honour it with a testament of our love colouring the sky."

To this day, it can be seen and is known as the rainbow, in honour of the lovers—Raeeni and Bouden, who created it.

Chapter Eight

Taha said, "That was a spellbinding story, and it reminded me that love is the most powerful emotion in the entire universe. I will always remember that story the next time I see a rainbow."

"Do you now agree a little about the influence of stories? They remain with us when all else is lost. Stories even have the power to transmute time and leave behind legacies," said Syun.

"Yes. I am beginning to believe. How true are your stories?" Taha asked.

"As true as you can imagine them to be," said Syun.

After a long pause, Taha asked, "How would you define love?"

"Love is the poetry of hearts. Love is the paradise of lands. Love is the pious of the spiritual. Love is the binding of your soul with that of another. Love takes many forms and many shapes, but it is the only power that has the inherent capacity to transform lives. If the whole world were to love instead of hate, then there would be no wars and we would all live in a beautiful age. When you love, your being vibrates at a higher frequency, sometimes connecting to the source. Have you ever felt that kind of love?"

After a long while, Taha replied, "I have not told anyone of this, but for some reason, I believe you will understand. I did, a few times feel what I call ' the great love', but that was when I was meditating and thinking of experiencing God. I felt a white light surround the room, and I felt my entire being covered from head to toe in an armour of bliss. I cried, but they were tears of joy for having been the recipient of such great love."

"Ah," said Syun, "what you speak of is a rare occurrence. Many devout Christians try to experience that, but very few actually do. So, you are indeed one of the few lucky ones. You must remember this power of love when you experience troubled times. But you are not doing so now, are you? Tell me why you stopped meditating."

Taha asked, "How did you know I stopped?"

"I know what there is to know," replied Syun.

After giving it some thought, Taha answered, "For a long time, I was in darkness. I felt no urge to do anything. My mind was blank, and my heart stopped experiencing joy at the sight of the sunrise. Circumstances had much to do with it, but mostly, I felt dead inside. I had given so much of myself to the world that I could not find the scattered pieces of it to fill my emptiness again. Perhaps if I had continued to meditate, I would have found it. But I was so uninspired that even that became a task."

"I will not ask you what your dark circumstances were because we are speaking of things of the light. But you must know that you are not the only one to suffer from the loss of inspiration. As children, the world is new to us, so everything becomes a source of wonder and curiosity, but when we become adults, we see too much, and we begin to look at the world through weary eyes. The things that once gave us joy no longer do so, and the things which can make us happy, we are unable to find it. But what is inspiration? Does it come from outside us or within?"

"When our souls are open, then the smallest things can touch them, causing inspiration," replied Taha.

"Exactly. When you know so much, you must also know that your soul, if you permit it, will always open the channels to inspiration. Let me tell you about the story of a little girl and the Inspheria incident," said Syun.

Chapter Nine

Story 4: The Inspheria Incident

There was once a time when there lived a little girl named Claie who walked on, filled with inspiration. She found it in the pitter-patter of rain. In the song of the summer breeze. In the passage of a book. In the light of the sun. In the babble of a brook. In curious corners, dreams, clouds, wishing wells, bubbles and smiles—in almost everything.

But when she grew up, everything changed. Her inspiration faded away like a painting that had lost its lustre with time. The only thing from her childhood that remained with her was that she talked to the moon.

One day, as she was having yet another fitful night of sleep, she felt herself lulled into a strange dream in which the moon was calling out to her. At first, she ignored it as nothing but fantasy. But the moon, which had heard all her stories, did not give up and persisted in calling her softly by her name.

"Claie. Claie, come to me," said the moon softly, again and again. When Claie opened her eyes and responded with a yes, she felt her spirit slowly being lifted from her body and travelling to the rooftop, where she most often sat and spoke to the moon. She watched her body curl in deep sleep, oblivious to what was happening. Claie floated through the air and reached the rooftop to see the silver-shining moon.

The moon told her, "You must come at once to where I take you."

"Are you really talking to me? Is this real?" An astonished Claie asked.

"You are now in a stage of wakeful sleep where anything is possible," replied the moon.

"Why are you calling me after all this time?" Claie asked.

"Inspheria is in trouble, and you must help it, as it has long helped you," replied the moon. "We don't have time for more words. Come at once."

So saying, the moon made a silver pathway from the sky to the earth. Using its gravitational pull, the moon lifted Claie from the rooftop onto the silver pathway. Away she went, floating into a vast space. Higher she floated until the earth was only a small dot. Suddenly, she was hurtling through space through a tunnel of silver light.

She saw glimpses of galaxies, asteroids, and meteorites. As Claie hurtled through, she felt herself transform into a little girl once again. In the sky full of stars, she saw a falling star and wished upon it for whatever task was at hand to come through, as she once did as a child. It had been a while since she had wished upon a star, let alone taken time to see one.

After a long while of hurtling, she saw a huge mass of land hovering in mid-air. It looked like a giant, inverted mountain suspended in space. Claie was softly placed at the edge of the cliff in front of a huge golden door. There was nothing else but dust in sight. Unsure of what to do next, Claie knocked on the door.

There was no response. She waited a while and knocked again. Still, there was no response. Suddenly, struck by a whim, she knocked in a pattern as she did on doors during childhood – thud, thud, thud, thud. The door opened with a giant swing and she stepped inside.

All at once, she was struck by a feeling of familiarity. It was like she knew this place from somewhere else. It was like the call of an old, familiar song, enveloping her in greeting. In front of her was a long bridge of flowers that led to the golden castle ahead. Below were luminescent waters filled with creatures she had never seen before—mermaids and flying fish. There were fountains of crystal-clear water. Butterflies were so big that one could ride them. Tall green trees laden with giant fruits. And a sky filled with marshmallow clouds and a big rainbow.

Almost abruptly, the music stopped, and her world turned grey. She saw that the bridge of flowers had withered. The water below was murky, and the fountains were relics. The castle that had just stood golden before her eyes was now muddy brown. The trees were barren, like still-standing skeletons. Claie rubbed her eyes and blinked again.

"It's faded," said a voice. "You saw what it was once, but after a few minutes, you saw the truth of what it has become now."

Claie whirled around to see who was talking to her. She saw a big brown butterfly at her side. The butterfly looked almost wise with its beady black eyes.

"But it used to be so beautiful! Why has it faded?" Claie exclaimed.

"You will know in time. For now, come; I will take you to the castle," said the butterfly.

Claie hopped on the butterfly's back, and it began its flight.

"I am Claie, by the way," she said.

"We all know. Welcome back. I am Arinon," replied the butterfly.

"What do you mean, you know? I haven't been here before. What is this place?" Claie said.

"What was once known has been forgotten," said Arinon. "Welcome to what is left of Insphirea."

"Insphirea! Why does that sound familiar?"

"It was your name for this place," said the Arinon.

"My name for it? But how? I told you I had never been here before," said Claie.

"Then why is everything familiar to you?" The butterfly asked. "Anyway, we have reached the castle. I will let the wise fairy, Aria, explain."

The butterfly rapped its antennae at the castle doors, and they opened. Claie's first impression of the castle interiors was one of washed-out beauty. What were once beautiful paintings now had dull edges; the regal statues were cracked;

the mesmerising murals of ethereal beings were no longer riveting. The throne stood empty.

But Claie could almost hear the sounds of laughter and music that once used to echo in the hallways of this lost paradise. But what stood out as clean and spotless was the figurine of Claie herself as a young child, sheathed in royal clothes and with a crown on her head.

"Is that me?" Claie asked.

"Yes. You used to rule this place," said Arinon.

"Who me? As a princess?" Squeaked Claie. "That cannot be. I live on Earth."

"But you are still on Earth, yet here as well. Aren't you? Insphirea used to be home to you once," said Arinon. "I just wanted you to see the statue, so you knew that you were well taken care of here."

"It seems to be the only thing that has withstood the test of time," said Claie.

"Yes. No one lives in the castle anymore. They all hide in the Garden of Light. Come, I will take you there," replied Arinon, with a touch of sadness in his voice. "Come, I will take you to Aria, the wise fairy."

With that, Arinon flew out of the castle windows and towards the Garden of Light. It was one small green patch in the otherwise creeper-filled forest. They flew in between the thick trees and lush flowers.

"How is this place still alive?" asked Claie.

"It is because you are," replied Arinon.

The butterfly flew over a flower field that was still in bloom. Arinon said, "This is the Field of Happiness, which requires the tears of sorrowful creatures to keep it alive and fertile."

"How can sorrow cause happiness?" Claie asked.

"Because without sorrow, one will never know happiness," replied Arinon. "Would you like to see the River of Rapture before we meet Aria?"

"Of course," said Claie.

The butterfly led Claie to the edge of the river, which was not as rapturous as she had expected it to be. A merman was waiting for her on a stone, and he said, "Welcome back, Claie. We have missed you so much. But you are still finding your feet here. Come, I will take you on from here. I am Anbu."

Pointing at a giant goldfish, he said, "And this is Nyoon, your ride."

"How can I breathe?" Claie asked.

"In Insphirea, all is possible," replied Anbu.

Claie sat on the goldfish and was taken into the river. She saw that its bed was filled with precious gems, corals, and pearls. As she was riding Nyoon, many creatures of the river came to greet her, and she was filled with a sense of fondness for them all. It was a whole other universe, with giant fish swimming along and merfolk strumming on their instruments, making amazing music. Anbu took her to a cave that was just about hidden.

"I know this place!" Claie exclaimed.

"Yes," replied Anbu. "This used to be your secret spot for all your treasures. Let's go inside."

The water cave was filled with many layers, which made for shelves. Along with them were picture books, globes, crystal balls, and a variety of seashells.

"Your treasures, which we have preserved," said Anbu.

"How come there are no precious stones here?" said Claie.

"When you were a child, the so-called riches did not matter to you. All you needed, something you called *found-forgotten-found* curiosities. Do not tell me you have changed."

"In my heart of hearts, I still think that I care about these real treasures," said Claie. "Even back on Earth, I go to the beach and pick up sea shells when I feel sad."

"It's good to know some things have not changed," said Anbu.

They went along the river for a while, with Claie observing and commenting and Anbu answering her questions.

Suddenly, Claie said, "I've been meaning to ask. What is all this dark matter that keeps floating by? It makes the river look dirty."

Anbu grimaced and said, "Well, truth be told, it is pollution — the pollution of your thoughts. The river was pristine and clean when you were a child but as you grew up, your thoughts grew murky, as did the river."

"It seems I have a special connection to this place," said Claie.

"Yes, you do," replied Anbu. "Perhaps it is time you go meet Aria, the wise fairy. Come, we'll take you back to the surface."

With that, they all returned to the spot where Arinon had left her. Claie bid Anbu farewell and solemnly said, "Thank you for everything. Will we ever meet again?"

"We will if your mind wills it," said Anbu as he dived back into the river.

Claie once again climbed up Arinon's back, and they both flew towards the Garden of Light. Little by little, creatures from the garden came out and watched her in delight. There was a heavy amount of whispering amidst the creatures, but it had been a long time, and so most of them were too shy to greet her in person.

As they went deeper into the garden, Claie could not help but admire the mysterious beauty of it all. There were flowers she had never seen before and trees she could not name; yet, they reminded her of paintings in a little drawing book she had once made as a child. As she was lost in her wonderment, she did not realise that Arinon had come to a halt in front of a tree.

"We're here," said Arinon, breaking her reverie.

Claie saw a huge tree that seemed to have flowers that looked like translucent, lit-up globes. It was a sight unlike anything she had ever seen before.

"Where are we?" Claie asked.

"Home of fairies," replied Arinon.

Claie stepped down from the butterfly's back and circled the tree a few times. She saw a swing that was attached to the branch at one side and felt the sudden urge to sit on it. As she swung from the swing, she broke into a melodic song that she hadn't sung since childhood. Almost at the end of her song, she saw a glitter of golden light spots appear in front of her face.

There was a flash of light, and she saw the most beautiful fairy she had ever seen. A creature so golden with wings made of cerulean blue. But it was the fairy's eyes that caught Claie's full attention, as they were so golden green that they almost looked into your soul.

"Hello," said Claie a bit uncertain in her awe.

"Hello, Claie. I am Aria. Sorry, I did not come to greet you, but I wanted you to see the truth for yourself," said the fairy.

"What is the truth?" Claie asked.

"As we are a bit rushed for time, I will tell you the truth as quickly as you need to know it. It is a good thing that you have accepted most of what you have seen without question. It goes to show that we have hope. Insphirea is a place created by you when you were a child, and you ruled over the Inspheirians with wonder and candour. Every time you were struck with inspiration, a part of this place grew and became what it is. This place belonged to a part of your mind, and as you nourished it, it grew."

"How wonderful a thought that is," remarked Claie. "No

wonder I feel like I know this place. Are all children able to do this?"

"Yes. Most children do. But many were not as powerful as you once were. When you were younger, we would even help other places created by other children to grow."

"So, why is it now not in full bloom like before?" Claie asked.

"Well, because you grew up and perception changed. For a long time, we helped each other to survive and thrive. A lot of what lives in this place came out of your head, Claie. But it has been a long time since you have nourished inspiration, whose nickname is Insphirea.

"You lost yourself, and so we lost ourselves. We have tried so hard to preserve this place, but you have grown to be a cynical adult, and that has made matters worse. Now, your darkness has grown and taken over most of this place, as you can see and it has decayed."

"So, if I change and believe in inspiration again, will everything be okay?" Claie asked.

"Well, your darkness took on a form and began living here, and the further you steered away from inspiration, the bigger it became. That is what has made the rivers murky with dirt, the songbirds stop singing, and the forest a wilderness. To make amends, you will have to defeat this creature that lurks in the dark."

"How can I do that?"

"Far at the edge of this land is a cave where lives Chalah, the Meditation Master. He could show you the way."

"How will I reach there?" Claie asked.

"You will ride upon Gatih." And with that, Aria whistled a tune into the thin air.

To her utmost surprise, Claie saw a unicorn come racing in front of her.

In answer to her unspoken question, Aria said, "Unicorns used to be your most favourite creature as a child and yes, he is real. The speediest mode of transport you will find here. He belongs to you. Now, rush and learn your lessons. I hope you will emerge victorious."

Claie mounted the unicorn, which galloped at the speed of light. It crossed valleys and mountains, but most of the land was barren, which made Claie realise how much inspiration she had lost. After days of riding, the unicorn came to a halt at the edge of a cave. Claie dismounted the unicorn and entered the cave.

It was a long and winding cave, and Claie felt a bit afraid that she might get lost. That's when she heard a voice in her head say, "Fear not, little one. Be brave. Let your soul guide you to me."

Taking tentative steps, Claie began to walk, and after a while, she found a large bat hanging upside down in the middle of the cave.

Claie spoke, "Hello Sir, I don't mean to interrupt, but I am looking for Chalah, the Meditation Master. Do you know where I can find him?"

"You have found him," replied the bat. "But you are yet to find yourself."

"What must I do to find myself?" Claie asked.

"Focus within," replied Chalah.

"How do I do that?" A bewildered Claie asked.

"Teach you, I will. How much you learn is up to you. Willing are you to learn?" The bat asked.

"Yes, I am willing," said Claie.

"Then enough it shall be," replied Chalah. "After gaining an understanding of Inspheria, you have to realise that the only way to save it is to cross the final barrier in a battle against fear. Fear is not a monstrous creature. Quite the opposite, it is very small and weak. It transforms into a monster based on how much fear it can induce in a person and feasts on the opponent by playing with his or her mind. The more the opponent fears the timid Fear, the stronger it grows."

"So, I will fight Fear," said Claie. "Will you tell me how?"

"Till you find focus within, you will sit still. You must learn to master your mind and control its wandering thoughts. The only thing you will do is eat one mushroom that grows within the cave, for each day you are here."

"Is that all?" Claie asked.

"Yes," replied the bat. "But you will soon find that sitting still is harder than you imagine. But begin you shall now."

"I will do it, for I have realised that I have been called here because, despite everything, a deep part of me still believes in things beyond what other humans do not," replied Claie.

"So be it," said Chalah.

So, Claie began to build her inner confidence, happiness, strength, focus, and more, guided and trained by Chalah, who gave her instructions, epiphanies, and wisdom to win against Fear and emerge victorious. Claie also fought hard to find her inner self because if she succeeded, then Insphirea would be reignited with inspiration and thereby, her world would be saved.

At first, she found concentrating very difficult, but the lack of food and the magic mushroom soon helped her find her pace. She learned to silence all her thoughts and find her centre by focusing on her breath. Soon, she could sit still for hours, lost within herself, and no matter how much noise the bat made, she remained undisturbed.

Sometimes, the bat would hit her with a stick, and she could still remain focused. Sometimes, he would flutter his wings and yet she remained focused. Soon, she found herself growing in her mind, with visions and thoughts that had never occurred to her before. One day, her focus was so intense that she created a small sphere of light in front of her and yet remained oblivious to it. The more she concentrated, the more the sphere of light began to glow.

That was when Chalah knew she was ready, and he gently woke her from her trance. Claie came to awareness gradually and her whole being was filled with a new sense of rigour.

"Ready you are now," said Chalah. "Go to the Room of Mirrors and face fear."

Claie bowed in reverence to her master and left for the entrance of the cave, where the unicorn awaited her.

"Let's go to the Room of Mirrors," she told Gatih.

Gatih had grown wings in the process of Claie's learning and so, he flew towards the Room of Mirrors, reaching there much faster than he would have galloped.

Claie stood in front of the room, readied her stance, and entered. The room was filled with mirrors of all kinds. They distorted her shape—some making grotesque forms of her, some mocking her, some mirroring her mind in a warped way. It was like the worst of Claie's fears were distorted across the mirrors and thrown back at her for her to see and cower. The Room of Mirrors was the one place where fear resided, and it had no sense of time. Claie's battle was to take place there.

Claie had to fight Fear. But how does one fight that which cannot be seen? It was at first an echo that took on life and size based on how much it could psyche out the opponent. The more fearful one got, the stronger the fear grew. Making one weak and defeated. But Claie had to train both her body and mind to defeat fear. She had learned meditation, exercise, positive thinking, and other techniques taught to her by Chalah. She had to find her true reflection to abate Fear.

Session 1: Hear No Fear

First, she heard whispers. *"You can't do this. Can you do this? You are weak and powerless. What if you fail? You are going to fail!"* The mirrors felt her darkest thoughts via fear and grew more grotesque every time she was struck by fear. This distorted her mind and blurred her identity until she did not know who she was anymore and didn't know what her reflections should be.

Claie began to fear being eternally trapped in a house of mirrors. Claie had to first overcome these voices. She began to say prayers in a voice louder than the Fearful voices. The louder her prayers were, the more the voices of Fear dulled. Finally, they faded away.

Session 2: See No Fear

Next, the mirrors made her scariest terrors appear as creatures—ghosts, monsters, and evil forces. She was supposed to battle them until they were vanquished. Claie sat still and closed her eyes in meditation. In doing so, she created mind avatars, which began to battle the forces that the mirrors showcased.

This happened on a parallel plane. The more she focused on her inner self, the more power the avatars took on, until they outgrew the creatures the mirrors had conjured and all lay slain after a bloody battle.

Session 3: Think No Fear

Next, Fear began to paralyse her mind through hypnosis and horror hallucinations, until she couldn't tell the difference between real and unreal. She did not know what she had to fight or what to ignore. She initiated the highest and most powerful form of meditation, Zen and created multiple avatars of herself. They created a protection shield around her mind, which empowered her to think without Fear and all the hallucinations got wiped away under the positive aura.

Session 4: Feel No Fear

Claie then went into a detached dynamic where nothing could reach her—body or mind. Her whole body began to vibrate, taking on an energy form, from somewhere else. The entire house of mirrors began to shake with her vibrations. All her avatars merged into her to create a more powerful force against fear. At that ultimate state of elevation, she saw which mirror was her true reflection. When she did so, all the other mirrors shattered into a zillion pieces, restoring Inspheria.

With a jumpstart, Claie woke up in her own bed on Earth but everything felt different. For the first time in a long time, she went to her notepad and penned a poem:

Windows to Worlds

Have you ever
Opened the door to your dreams.
With a key to inspiration,
And listened to your heart?
Ran away from nothing.
Towards no destination, in no direction.
Just to chase the wind?
Swam in the ocean.
Seeking mermaids and myths.

Held a shell and awaited a story?
Whispered a wish into a tree;
And waited for fairies to reply.
Went searching for belief;
In the forest of faith?
Looked for faces in the clouds;
And christened them with names?
Have you ever
Borrowed threads from a spider.
To weave a web of wonder;
And catch visions in it?
Got lost in your imagination.
Painting your thoughts
And wording your silence?
Planted a seed of hope.
For it to reach far and high;
And make a passage to the sky?
Have you ever
Written a letter to God;
And set it sail on the sea.
Sipped on water to taste wine.
Or picked pearls from pebbles?
Mistaken coincidence for a miracle.
And read a sign in the stars?
Have you ever?

Claie looked up to the moon and smiled, and in her mind's eye, she saw a blossoming Inspheria.

Chapter Ten

Taha said, "Did that really happen to her in the story, or was it just her dream? Like a subconscious metaphor?"

Syun said, "It was a story. What does it matter, real or not real? The purpose of any story is to grasp its meaning."

"So, we all need to have the spirit to keep inspiration alive?" Taha queried.

"Most of us do, but we fail to believe that. When you lose inspiration—stop, stay still, and watch the world. There is so much around us that can inspire; the colours of a flower, the grand stance of a tree, a bird in flight, a star-kissed sky, a simple trickle of water, the shape of someone's eyes, the feet of a baby, and the colours in the sky. Look at nature. Look at people. Observe, retain, and remember. But we need a child-like, not childish, attitude towards life. Surrender to the beauty of living and stop worrying so much. What is and what will be, will be."

"I read somewhere that if the sight of sunrise does not bring a man joy, then he is as good as dead. If such is the loss of inspiration, then what does one do?" Taha asked.

"One must stop and start again. When one does not feel in his heart, that means he has been treading the wrong path for a long time and has lost contact with his inner soul. All he can do is stop wherever he is and start again. When man stops enjoying simple things, it is time to pause, reflect, and realise. Self-realisation happens in stillness, solitude, and silence," replied Syun.

"What if he cannot do so?" Taha asked.

"There is no such thing as a *cannot*. Everything is possible when we put our minds to it. Let me tell you a story."

Chapter Eleven

Story 5: Imogene's Nation

Once upon a time, on the Earth of the olden days, reality was the only philosophy and people just accepted the world as it was. They followed what their parents taught them and lived a life of routine. Mundane conditioning in an uncreative world.

People dressed similarly, and everything looked alike. Uniformed clothes, houses, and patterns but their surroundings were still beautiful. However, there was no art, no poetry or stories. Just reality as it was, governed by the Summit.

There lived a couple far away, near the banks of a river in a deserted forest. They both longed for a child but were ordained not to have one and they prayed to the gods to give them one with solemn sincerity. One day, as the man went fishing on the river, his net caught a silver egg. Amused and bewildered by it, he took it home and kept it in a bucket of water.

After fifteen long days, the egg broke to give birth to a child that was half human and half mythical. She had the form of a human, except for her feet, which were like the fins of a fish and had silver wings growing from the shoulder blades. Tiny though she was, the couple knew she could not be kept in a bucket.

Therefore, they built a huge tank of water for her and kept her in it. They loved her as if she were their own child and they named her Imogene. They tried to keep the baby girl hidden from the rest of the world, which they knew would not accept her.

Imogene was a mischievous and playful child who was never in need of company, as she lived in her own world. She saw the world in her own way and often came up with ideas that no one else could ever dream of. Her parents left her to pursue her individuality, as they understood the uniqueness of their child but Imogene never thought of herself as unusual, because she was accepted at her home.

As she grew older, she realised she had strange powers—if she willed her mind to do so, she could create her feet and walk upon them. She could breathe the open air and roam about the earth as a human. She could conjure up little tricks in her mind and will them to be true. Such as a feast-laden table, sparks of fire for the fireplace, and even a tail for her parents.

As she grew older, she could no longer be contained in the aquarium created for her by her parents. So, they let her live in a river near the house, giving her both love and freedom. But as time flew by, they realised she was more than odd. She was observant and thought more of things, outside the general perception and was always in pursuit of why.

She created fantastical figments and things that did not seem to be of this realm. She was a curious little girl, always pondering things and eager to explore worlds beyond her own. So, her parents warned her never to venture past the waterfall at the edge of the river, for humans lived in the congregation beyond.

But one day, Imogene wandered away from home, easily slipping her parents' vigilance. She swam to the edge of the waterfall, eager to seek new wonders. Despite her elders' warnings and the doubt in her heart, she swam down anyway and found herself falling. She surfaced in the shallow waters of a different sea. As she was just finding her bearings, she got caught in the fishing net of two humans, who took her to the Summit to see what became of her.

When the Summit saw and heard the way she talked and thought, they assumed that she was of another world, despite her protestations otherwise. Her thoughts and the imagined worlds she described were blasphemous to them. Colours, paintings, melodies, rhythms, and musings, didn't mean anything of significance to them.

But Imogene was oblivious to their mistrust, for she had never seen anything beyond her house and river. She was as fascinated with humankind as they were with her. The decree in the decision was to put her in a ginormous glass bowl and make her a part of a travelling show so the world could see her.

It is said that a fish grows only as big as its bowl—the smaller the bowl, the smaller the fish. The bigger the bowl, the bigger the fish would be. So, the Summit decided that she must be put in a glass bowl case with the logic that if her head expands with her body, God knows what will come of it.

So, if her body and head were prevented from growing bigger, so would her thoughts. But the mind is more than the body and so, even in her containment, her thoughts flew, especially when pressured.

At first, it was fun for Imogene, as she saw so many shades of the world and absorbed everything. She watched them as they watched her, each intrigued by the other. But what she did not know about the Summit's notion was that amusements would pass and be confined to colourless reality again.

Even though her body was contained, her mind could not be. Refusing to be trapped in the box, Imogene created her own world. One of colours, unseen things, places of hope, times unknown, inventive and original. Her creations floated free into the far world, colouring and transforming it and the Summit was alarmed because the reality they knew was no longer the same.

Soon, Imogene felt confined and sad in her cage and begged to be set free but the Summit was now fearful of her identity and capabilities. They had seen her make people dream of things that did not exist. They had seen her create colour in an otherwise monochrome world. And the more they grew older, the stronger her abilities seemed to be. So, they shut her off from the travelling glass bowl and put her in prison.

They kept her in a tight glass cubicle of water for fear that if her body grew, so would her powers. The Summit had no notion of things like the mind. In her confinement, Imogene grew dull and listless; her fins faded to grey and her mermaid tail grew powerless. She wept for hours and looked at the single vision she had to see the moon.

Her powers began to fade, and the Summit was thrilled that their plan was working. This went on for a few years and Imogene became another fish in another pond, but her mind never stopped working.

One day, Imogene lifted her head to the moon, thought of the freedom with her parents, and felt a connection with something more. Something higher. That was when a young boy entered her room and stayed at the door. He looked frightened. They both stayed silent for a while and then, seeing that he would not be hurt, the young boy stepped forward and threw her some food. Seeing the young boy's innocent eyes, Imogene felt the loss of her own innocence and said, "What is your name, boy?"

Alarmed at first, the boy said nothing, but then he looked into her eyes and saw a sense of kinship there. "I am Kay. They have banned me from the Summit because I paint."

"Why is painting a bad thing?" Imogene asked.

"That's because they say it's a waste of time," said Kay. "Another friend of mine tries to write poetry, but he loses his will because the world does not understand. In this bleak world, thoughts are hard to come by. Before we become adults, we conform to the Summit's way of living."

There was silence for a while as Imogene ate, and the boy stared at her in wonder.

Suddenly he said, "You have wings. Why do you not fly away?"

Imogene replied, "My wings are not yet fully formed, and they also have a lock on this cage."

"Do you feel sad?" The boy asked.

"I feel suffocated," replied Imogene. "Like my mind is unable to function."

"Maybe that is because you don't let it. Imagine what could happen if you power it to your full potential."

The boy's words struck a chord within Imogene and she smiled for the first time in many years. Automatically, her wings grew a little more silver.

"See, if that can happen with just a smile; imagine what could happen if you really put your mind to it."

Suddenly, there was a commotion outside.

"What's taking you so long, boy?" A loud, angry voice said.

The boy looked frightened and ran outside. The Summit guards stopped him at the door and gave him a heavy whipping.

Watching this, Imogene's heart turned resolute. *No world should function like this*, she thought. *People deserve the gift of having their minds heard.*

After whipping the boy, they put Imogene in a tighter cage, making her escape tougher. The cage was small and restrictive. It barely gave her room to move. They put her in the centre of the town square as a warning for those who defied the Summit. The older men and women looked at her with disgust but the young people looked at her with sympathy and slight expectation.

They had heard stories of a being that could change monochrome into colour. Watching the young eyes, Imogene made the decision that she would be unlike anyone who had prevailed at the Summit before. Despite the cage constricting her body, she shut her eyes and grew still. She ignored the watchers and the world and looked within her mind.

She focused on her mind and the worlds it created. She absorbed the source and went into a trance. She went to the cosmos, the place of her creators, the land of the unthinkable, the place of dreams, and the space without fear. She crossed oceans and deserts in her mind. The universe complied and sharpened her wings.

She flew in her mind to the cosmos and took the energies from there. She flew to dark spaces and took shadows from there. She flew across illusions and took magic from there. Soon, people could see that the box was filled with golden flecks of light and that Imogene was glowing.

One day, the box was no longer able to contain the power of her thoughts and was shattered. The fragments of her mind filled the Summit world with new hues and shades. The monochrome world faded into a watercolour painting.

Her wings grew to full, silvery strength. Before flying away, she bestowed upon mankind a boon—her nation, Imogene's nation, or what we now call, with words abridged '*imagination*'.

It took only a little of her creations to fill the earth; the rest remained lingering, waiting for humans to pick them up and reach them. Not everyone is privy to her nation; only those who have opened their mind's eyes — those who try to break free of their internal fish-bowl world to see and believe in the beyond, become part of her world. The more liberated one's mind, the greater their entrance to Imogene's nation, or as it is now called, imagination.

Chapter Twelve

Taha quietly contemplated the story. After a while, she asked Syun, "Do you think this world is God's imagination?"

Syun replied, "It is a fun way to think of this world, isn't it? When a painter gets inspired, he fills up a canvas. When a writer gets inspired, he fills pages. In the same manner, maybe God was inspired and used the biggest platform to create a world so vast that it mesmerises the mind."

Taha laughed and replied, "Maybe God got lonely. Imagine being alone in a limitless galaxy. As beautiful as it may have been, maybe God too craved some company. That's why I think He made us and this world is his reflection."

"Oh, I think God was at his creative best when he made this earth into what it is. Scientists may say things like evolution, which is also true, but isn't it a more interesting way to think of it all as God's creation out of imagination? It gives a humane perspective of God," Syun replied.

"When I was younger, I used to think that God sculpted us out of clay. I used to think that we went to him with a list of what we wanted to look like, and he made us look that way. That is why no single person is the same. I used to imagine the immensity of God's imagination," said Taha.

"Do you think we are alone in this universe?" Syun asked.

"I think that it is hugely egoistic of us to think so. Often at night, when I used to stare at the stars, I used to think that there were other beings across galaxies doing the same thing as well. So, I don't think that we are alone in this big, bright, and beautiful universe."

Taha paused and continued, "Also, if we do tend to notice, that is why the concept of what we call 'aliens' exists. Of course, we have made it into a sci-fi norm, but what if there were other creatures who were also curious about contacting us and perhaps even had answers for us? Sometimes, I think we have limited ourselves to one world when we could have had so many more."

"This is true. You are a seeker then, for things greater?"

"I think I have always been searching for answers to things that I do not understand or cannot even comprehend."

"That should be the true quest of mankind—to believe that something higher exists and be in constant pursuit of it. Not everyone has to be a great meditator or divine explorer. But having a burning question of 'who am I?' is a prerequisite to understanding the purpose of life."

"I have been wondering who I am for the past years. For the first few years of my life, I was defined by what others thought of me. But that is not who I am. I once wrote a poem about it. Would you like to hear?"

"With pleasure."

Taha thus began to quote the poem:

Who am I?
Who am I?
A star fallen from the sky?
Who am I?
Do I get to ask why?
I am here.
Here
Do I know what this really is?
Am I to believe scientific discoveries?
Am I to believe religious theories?
Can someone help me, please?
Am I just another human?
Am I my own reflection?
If I'm here now, where was I before?
Why can't I remember anymore?
Do we all come with some purpose?
Or are we all clowns in His circus?
If I am known by what I think,
Then I am only my mind.
If I am known by what I feel,
Then I am only my heart!
But am I just my body in part?
Or am I what holds it together?
Am I the child of my mother?
A friend, a lover, a sister?
If relations define who I am,

Who defines my relationships?
Do I get to put it together?
The pieces of my character?
Or is it built into my system?
As I go and when I come
Am I the face I see in the mirror?
Or is it the voice of the soul I hear?
Am I the breath that keeps me alive?
Am I willing to survive?
Am I a soul waiting to be free?
If I am a part of God,
Who, then, is He?
Who am I?
A body, a soul, an illusion?
Who am I?
My own or someone else's perception?
Who knows who we are here?
We take our lifetime to discover.
By the time I know the answer,
Does it really matter?
Who am I here?

After listening to the poem, Syun said, "You are asking all the right questions, and in time, with persistence, you will find the right answers."

"Do you know the right answers?"

"Through years of meditation, I have found some answers, but those are for me to know and for you to find out yourself.

All I will tell you is this. You are not your body, but your soul, which always belongs to God."

"Do you think everyone gets the chance to experience God?" Taha asked.

"Yes. Most definitely. But one has to exercise caution of the senses and not talk about their journey to everyone, for there are those who get jealous or do not understand."

"Why would anyone get jealous?" Taha queried.

Syun replied, "Those who are truly noble, do not. But not all have the same bounty of *Karma* and the piousness required to please God. Most people prefer a shortcut and get dejected when their prayers are not answered. In this state of frustration, watching another person rise brings out an envy that can be dangerous. Let me tell you a story."

Chapter Thirteen

Story 6: The Sunshine Healer and the Sunshine Stealer

There was once a time when two people, wanted to fly into the sky. They were not mere earthly mortals but two stars who had chosen to fall from the sky to experience human life. They were destined to be darkness dispensers who had been born to provide succour to the earth's sorrow and suffering.

One was a boy named Thorne, who was charismatic and clever. He was made of physical grit and guts. The other was a girl called Skye, who was sensitive and serene. She was made of inner strength and kindness. As willed by forces unknown, they both met and fell deeply in love.

Their passion was so profound that they forgot their innate purpose and became content living as earthlings. They spent their days helping those in need, feeding dogs and cats, laughing at Fate's jokes and spinning stories of what life would be like when they grew older.

One day, however, their idyllic lives came to an end when time brought them a reminder of their past in separate but similar dreams. They both dreamt that one of them would be chosen as the leader to help the world if they accepted the challenge. To realise their true potential, reaching the sun was their immortality—their invincibility.

Upon awakening, Thorne remained silent but Skye told him of her dream. It was only then that he came forth and said that he had dreamt something similar. As they had done everything together thus far, they both discussed how to pursue this dilemma, as they both wanted to win but also wanted the other to win.

It was decided that they would have to follow their respective journey to attain what they needed. “Like two river banks that follow the same course, always parallel but never together,” he said.

“Like two rivers that lead into the same ocean,” she said.

In order to seek the sun, the boy, who had a scientific mind, began to use technology to create a set of wings. He read avidly about the intellectual pursuits of past inventors and theories of quantum physics and worked on his wings. He was fast in his fervour and secretive in his experiments. He worked with logic.

The girl had a spiritual mind and prayed patiently for the time her inner wings would form through meditation and creation. Then she, too, could fly. She painted and wrote songs about her visions, for an uplifted humanity. She sang hymns to the moon and sun, and read philosophical books on achieving a higher state of body and mind. She worked with love.

From time to time, they encouraged each other in their paths and progress. One night, as they were standing under the stars, playing their game of creating constellations, Skye felt a sense of foreboding sadness.

"Time and us—it will never be the same again," she said. Although he was aware that she had an aptitude for intuition, Thorne tried to console her and promised her, that neither time nor space could ever come between them. At that moment, they saw a shooting star flash across the sky and they both made a silent wish.

"What did you wish for?" Thorne asked.

"That your wishes come true. What did you wish for?"

"That whatever you wish for comes true."

They both smiled sadly and sat under the stars for a long time, holding hands and hope nursing their hurting hearts.

As the days flew by, they both continued working on their 'wonder wings'. Skye soon began to feel the first sprout of her wings bestowed upon her by higher powers. She felt clarity in her thoughts and courage in her heart. She used that to focus her will on her wings to make them grow mightier and more magical.

However, Thorne, with his technological technique, began to grow frustrated. No matter what he tried, he always found a core quotient missing but did not know what it was. When her wings were half-grown, Skye could not contain her excitement and ran to her lover to show him her success.

With honesty, she described the 'heavenly' voices that had guided her to her growth and the methods she had used to conjure them. That was when Thorne realised that what he needed was the Creator's light, which he could not summon for himself as she did because he had mixed his path with worldly vices. But mostly because his logical mind refused to keep an open perspective and believe in the magic of possibilities.

Unknown to her, Thorne began to get envious. He always believed that he was the superior being and deserved to be the first to fly to the sun. It was not only ambition that motivated him but also a strong desire for immortality and its immense power. He knew that love was both Skye's fortitude and fragility, as she desired not power but a limitless kind of love, which she believed she could share with the world and eventually heal it.

So, Thorne studied his science and used it to create a hypnosis method by which he could control Skye's mind and slowly obtain her light for his wings. He knew that for him to get stronger, she would have to get weaker. He was unaware of the cause and consequence of his actions, as he was too focused on pursuing a glorified and selfish goal. He began to manipulate her mind to harness the secrets of her 'natural' abilities for his advancement and started stealing her shine.

Skye was a strong spirit, but she had led herself to a higher state of consciousness so that her wings could develop. That meant that she was open to forces of all kinds. Just as the good heard her calling, so did the evil, since both exist in a strange balance in worlds above and below. As Thorne began to steal her shine, little by little, she felt herself and her world grow darker.

She experienced a weakening of her spirit, as well as the deterioration of her dark powers. Her intuition told her that something was wrong but she took it as a part of the adaptation process, never once thinking that someone could be harming her. She held onto her bold belief, but try as she did, her wings seemed to have stopped forming.

With the protection of her light ebbing, she felt her mind was no longer her own and began to see the dark entities that lived in the parallel realm. Half-rotting bodies, gruesome ghosts, and demonic beings began to pervade her self-sphere. Their torturous voices taunted her abilities until she felt defeated and began losing her sense of self-worth and belief.

Disoriented and in deep despair, she sought the protection of Thorne, who did give her refuge in his home but no longer in his heart, which had grown greedy in its power pursuit. After staying with him after a period of separation, she found that he too had changed and was now cruel.

His harsh manner and wicked words wounded her gentle heart until she felt herself filled with sadness. She stopped meditating, singing, dancing, and even smiling. She grew fragile, fighting forces that mocked and mind-played with her while he grew stronger. So, days went by with her lost in chaos and confusion while he grew closer to finishing his wings.

One night, left alone at home, as it had become the regular case, Skye, who was unable to sleep, began to pace about the house, with its walls whispering memories of happier times. She remembered how they had danced and played together. She remembered how she used to sleep on his arm—her pillow.

She remembered most of all the look of love in his eyes for her, which now seemed filled with a brooding blackness when he watched her. There was a rustle in the ruins of her mind and her steps took her towards his workroom, which was surprisingly unlocked. Although he had banned her from entering it, she entered anyway, drawn almost as if by another power.

The place was a mess. There were papers all over the place and a variety of gadgets strewn about. At the centre of it all was a magnificent pair of almost finished wings. She leaned in to look closer and a flash of light caught her eye, making her stumble backwards. As she did, she hit a cupboard, and a pile of papers cascaded on her.

Afraid that it would be enough to trigger his newfound temper, she quickly began collecting them to put them back in place. But an illustration made her pause. It was a crude sketch of a meditating female figure with her third eye open. What intrigued her was that the light emitting from it was being channelled onto another figure—a male.

She began to read the notes and realised that this was an illustration for him, to make her shine. More illustrations showed his plan to take all the light from the earth, spread darkness and create the strongest set of wings that would take him beyond the sun. All at once, everything made sense.

She did not know how he had done it, nor did she care. But knowing him, she knew he would cease at nothing till he conquered it all.

Betrayed and bewildered, she ran out of the door, tears streaming down her face. She ran blindly until she reached her own home. She cried for a long time, unable to believe what she had just seen. After her tears of heartbreak halted, she began to think things through.

Her love for him led her to let him do so, believing in his love for her. But now the time had come when she had to decide. She wondered if her love could stop him and fill him instead with her shine, but she knew that no light could be let in if a person did not choose to allow it.

She recalled the boy she had loved, before the man he had become and knew that this dark destruction had to be stopped. She knew that darkness could only be countered with love and light. So, at the first ray of dawn, she went to a deserted beach. For the first time in a long time, she sat in meditation with a laser-like focus on her Creator and the spirits of her home.

She detached herself from the pain of this world. She began to power herself with a strong shine of the Creator's light. As she prayed, she summoned all of Thorne's dark energies and intentions towards her. As they answered and became part of her, Thorne felt a change occur within him.

He felt the power of her decision and felt his aggressive ambition shed away as if it was never there, and he heard his soul scream for the love he had forsaken. In a telepathic thought, he realised that he was losing the only person he had ever really cared about and willed her to stop and return.

Skye felt the shift in Thorne's heart, but she knew that she was on an unstoppable path. The dark energies were swirling about her, and they could no longer have their place in this realm. She had made her choice, and it was a sacrifice. She thought of Thorne one last time and then said a final prayer to the good powers and her wings.

She stilled her mind, silenced her aching soul and continued to power herself. At first, sparkling lights began to surround her and soon, her whole being was orbiting in a sphere of luminous lights. She was lifted off the ground, and as she continued to orbit in light, within her shoulder blades, released an enormous pair of Icarian wings.

As they formed with pain and purity, she flapped them to fly. As she ascended above mortal existence, for one moment, she turned around to see all that she was leaving behind—to see the human whom she had loved and who had left her behind. Then, with her head high in determination, she flapped her mightier wings to rise.

The sun, which was a dot, grew bigger and the world, which she loved, grew into a dot. Still, she flew faster, as it would take all her strength to reach the sun, to break beyond the barriers. She was motivated to fly to the sun by her agony and her mission. She was unable to see as she approached closer due to its blinding brightness. Her wings began to burn with the sun's heat, but she continued using her love as power.

She could feel the flames blistering her being, but her tears of farewell assuaged them and she crossed the boundary of normal flight and set forth into the scorching sun. She flew into it, merging herself into it. As she did so, her skin and wings began to burn, as did all the black forces she had carried along with her and there was a big, bright light across the sky.

As the last of the darkness was dispelled, she burst into many pieces of ash and her soul joined the sun, the One. Her ashes sprinkled down towards the earth, transforming into particles of light that settled down on the high-tech wings made by Thorne. The moment they landed on it; the wings changed into cosmic ones.

They became the fibre, the vein and the core of the wings he wanted, each made up of a little piece of her true shine. Thorne finally had the wings he wanted, but at that moment, he knew that he had lost her forever. He had turned from the sunshine stealer to the sunshine healer but at a cataclysmic cost.

Even though Thorne had wings, he knew that he could never reach the sun like she did. To this day, he goes from person to person, using his wings to direct the sun's light to worthy people, trying to shine and heal their sorrows. He hoped within himself that one day, he would be able to spread enough light, to join her in the sun.

Chapter Fourteen

"In love too, wisdom is needed, to be careful," said Taha.

"Yes. When we are children, we are pure, but greed's descent is easy. We want what others have and are not satisfied with what we are," said Syun.

"I feel like your stories have opened my mind and transformed my soul," said Taha.

"That was my purpose of meeting you," replied Syun.

"What makes me special enough?" Taha asked.

"The fact that you in your heart, hold on to things which most have lost belief in," said Syun.

"Despite all the trials I have been through, I still believe. I think of God as my eternal friend," said Taha.

"That is the right path. You will still face difficulties, but knowing is enough," said Syun.

"How do I deal with these difficulties?" Taha asked.

"It would help to think of your life as a book," said Syun.

"You mean like an autobiography?"

"Of sorts, but not really."

"Oh, the metaphor again. You do a lot of those, don't you?"

"It makes explaining easier."

"So, life as a book–meaning?"

"When you pick up a book, you don't really know what it is about. You begin reading, and soon, each chapter brings a new twist, an unexpected character, and a new plot. What keeps you reading is the anticipation of what might be revealed in the next chapter. A lot doesn't make sense, and you are filled with questions.

"But with each chapter you read, it makes more sense and finally, you reach the end of the book. In my stories, you understand the purpose of the characters and the meaning of the story, and you are satisfied. Now, you can put away the book and search for something new. If you think of life as a book, then it begins when you are born. Each phase of your life then becomes a new chapter.

"Some chapters are boring, some bleak, some exciting, but what keeps us going is the knowledge that at the turn of a page, a new chapter might begin. If you stop reading a chapter that feels so dreary, then you will never know what lies in the rest of the story. Some people only read the chapters of life and miss the whole book," said Syun.

"I used to pretend that I was in a movie," said Taha.

"Ah. It is also a way for angels to integrate you with a higher realm. But you have to be careful to be clean," said Syun.

"Clean?"

"To deal only in love, which is what the angels respond to, and not hate," said Syun.

"I don't think I deal in hate, but sometimes, it is hard to know," replied Taha.

"Just to be clear, let me tell you a story," said Syun.

Chapter Fifteen

Story 7: Love and Hate

Once upon a time, twins were born called Love and Hate. Both possessed the ability to make Potions of desire, drawn from their inner selves. They were best friends and often went about striking arrows of love into well-suited mortal creatures with a Passion Potion. They often sat on the clouds and watched different people meet each other and fall in love. As time went by, they both grew up, happy in their task of making the lives of random strangers coincide.

One day, both of them watched an earthly mortal who was a very beautiful woman. What made her so beautiful was that she had a kind, generous, and loving heart. She was kind to everyone around her—both humans and animals. She watched the moon and smiled at the sun. She grew flowers in her garden and planted seeds of hope.

For a while, they looked for another earthly mortal to bind her with, but Love and Hate felt that no one was good enough for this maiden. By watching her, they both fell in love with her. Being the best of friends, they decided to make themselves known to her and let her choose with whom her heart aligns.

Little by little, they made their appearance in her life. Love chose the path of charm. He left flowers by her window, appeared to her in beautiful dreams and made her heart listen to music. Hate chose the path of magic—he left precious stones by her doorstep, dazzling clothes in her wardrobe, and made her rich with desire. The maiden had a fair heart, and she did not want to hurt anyone, but she felt that there was a darker side to Hate, which scared her and thus, she chose Love.

For a few years, everything was all right, and Hate was content that his brother was happy, for he realised that he did not love the maiden as much as his brother did. But his ego was hurt by the rejection, although he did his best to hide it. Gradually, their laughter began to grate on his nerves.

Their happiness made him jealous and their passion made him restless. Without his knowledge, the arrows that he started to make began to get tainted by his inner self and people for the first time experienced something that was the opposite of love. They began to consume the darkness that was festering in Hate's heart, and the world began to grow dark. Soon, Hate began to try to strike the dark arrow into the maiden's heart.

Love was oblivious to what was happening, but he soon realised that his maiden was not smiling as much as before. Her songs were off-key, and her eyes had grown sad. He tried his best to make her cheerful, but nothing he did made a difference to her emotions. Blue with bewilderment, he approached the Soul Sorcerer, who had a magic mirror that looked into people's souls. That was when Love found out that his brother Hate was poisoning the maiden and as many people as he could with dark magic.

Furious, he set out to meet his brother to try to convince him of the error of his ways. But Hate had grown stronger and was adamant in his belief that he was right. Having understood that it was impossible to change his brother's mind, Love simply did what he did best—he began to shine stronger. He used all of his energy to make arrows of light that would penetrate the deepest and darkest of hearts.

Slowly, Love's endurance and effort made the difference, and people began to lose their hate. When Hate realised what was happening, that he was growing powerless, he chose the darkest path to break Love's work. But he found that as long as people held onto love, it was impossible for hate to penetrate their souls. He realised that Love was stronger than him.

Filled with rage, he went into the deepest abyss to plot a dramatic return one day. To this date, Hate is still there, waiting for its turn to corrupt people's minds and hearts. He lurks quietly in the dark, waiting for even the slightest chasm in people's minds to seep his own darkness into them. That's why people must strive harder to hold on to love, no matter what.

Love can make people meet but it is up to them to sustain and strengthen it. Hatred is always waiting for a chance to fester in weakened minds.

Chapter Sixteen

Syun spoke, "Hate exists, as does love, within us and around us. It is up to us to decide who we permit into our lives. One can easily undergo a destructive change. Both are equally powerful. But remember the Tailor of Fate and his bequest to mankind? This is where we get to exercise it."

Syun sought the quietness for a moment and then said, "Time is running short for us, and I have two more stories yet to tell you. So, let me begin another, which is linked to this—it is about happiness."

"So be it," said Taha.

Chapter Seventeen

Story 8: The Happiness Story

Once upon a time, God decided to bestow on Earth the gift of happiness. He made it into a beautiful box and sent it down with one condition; those who used the box for its gifts needed to put one happy thought back into it. For a long time, people followed the tradition and kept passing the box on. They used it not only for themselves but for others as well.

However, as time passed, people got so consumed in their happiness that they forgot to put one thing back into it, which is a selfish act. Little by little, the box used up its magic and got worn out until one day, it was discarded in the bin.

There sat the box, torn and tired. It turned to God and said, "All my life, I did what you asked. I shared the happiness you put into me, but mankind was so unkind that, at one point, they forgot to repay. Now, what do you have to say?"

So moved was God by the box's pain and plea that he wished all the people who did not give back one trace of happiness to the box, must return it threefold. Suddenly, people found themselves wishing for other people's happiness three times.

When they did so, the box became a beautiful maiden. She went on to be the person who bestowed happiness on all those she deemed worthy. But what happened to the people who did not share their happiness? After paying the price, they learned their lesson.

Chapter Eighteen

"True happiness is what you create within yourself and it positively affects lives around you. You are the master of your own happiness."

"How does one calm the mind?" Taha asked.

"Still your mind and concentrate on the nothingness of everything. Let sounds of the world and life surround you. Let your mind take over and guide the sounds into calmness, to be content. After a while, they will. Then seek the inner world within yourself, through meditation and transcend the outer world," replied Syun.

"Is it easy?" Taha asked.

"It is easy enough but one needs hope. It is not through mere theology that one attains God but through the knowledge of Soul," said Syun. "Do you want to try it now?"

"Yes," said Taha. "With you."

They both closed their eyes and sat in the lotus position. Taha focused her eyes on her inner mind and let everything surround her. She heard the sound of the wind, the birds chirping and the lap of the lake, but slowly, everything blended into one sound. She focused harder. She felt her body grow warm despite the wind.

She once said the name of the God she most believes in. Suddenly, everything became calm. She could feel her breath, but she was concentrating on her breathing. She felt the sun on her face. She felt tranquil. There was silence in her being and mind. Little dots of light began to surround her, swarming her in an uplifted atmosphere.

She could see them even though her eyes were closed. They surrounded her until she was surrounded by an aura of light. But then she focused on Syun, and the strangest thing happened. All she could see was a brilliant form of light emanating from him and forming his outline. Suddenly, she felt such bliss like she never had before and knew with certainty that had witnessed Divine Awakening.

Time grew static, and they may have sat there for minutes or hours. Still statues of serenity, but then she heard Syun's voice flood through her being.

"Yes, embedded beneath your layer of confusion is a Soul that hopes. That is all that God needs to call you to Himself."

"I still cannot speak, for silence has taken over my soul."

"Then let me end it with a story worthy of hope," said Syun.

Chapter Nineteen

Story 9: How Hope Came to Be

Once upon a time, long before now, Hope used to be called *Hop*. Why? Because a rabbit called Hop used to hop from the moon, where it stayed and give things to people who needed them. The moon had once given him special seeds that could grow into beautiful flowers when touched by moonlight.

Every night, Hop would tend his garden of flowers and pluck the fully blossomed ones because they too were special. When humans smelled the scent of it, they were intoxicated with Hope. People used to go and get a little of what they needed when they needed it, and it filled their hearts with wonder drugs for a little while—like moon medicine, moonshine, and madness.

Hop had the quality of being strangely addictive. People slowly started getting addicted to it and became more demanding about how and when they needed it. They stopped enjoying the beauty it would bring and forgot that they had to hold on to the memory during the tough times. Instead, the lines for Hope grew longer and longer until this greed started causing Hop's flowers to wither and lose their magic potion.

Now, the humans who were addicted to Hope began to take their wrath out on the poor rabbit, who still believed that he could fulfil the poor people's wishes, with the help of the moon. But the moon saw the way that people were treating the rabbit and stopped laminating the flowers with its light. Hence, the flowers lost their special magic.

Years went by and nothing happened. People began to suffer from a futile sense of listlessness and began to grow sad. Seeing this, the rabbit grew sad as well, for he had spent his life in the service of hope.

One day, the rabbit grew old and nothing had happened to his flowers, so he prayed to the moon for a boon. Not for him but for others. The moon and its Creator had watched him every night for years. So, God took his flowers, put everything into them and sent them out into the world. That's how it came to be known as *Hop (e)—Hop + Everything.*

Now, it is up to people to keep it and it is up to us to discern what kind of Hope to hold on to. That's also why there is a rabbit on the moon. To remind us that no matter who or what you are, with a little Hope, you can reach the greatest heights and the farthest distance.

Chapter Twenty

"The story of Hope is the final one I shall give you, as Hope is all it takes for us to move forward in life," said Syun.

"I shall remember that God put Everything into Hop and made Hope, and hold on to it," said Taha.

"When none else shall remain, let there be hope in your heart."

"So, I may always find the way to return," finished Taha.

"Now," said Syun, "go wash away your old life in the lake, wash away the years of burden and worries you have carried with you and emerge as new."

"I do not know how to thank you," said Taha.

"Remember my stories, share them and live a changed and a better life. That will be enough. Now go. It is time," said Syun.

Taha proceeded towards the cool, calm lake and dipped herself in it. As she did so, she felt her heart grow light and her body warm. Her mind was crystal-clear and her heart felt a flutter of promise—that with Will and Wonder, she could be anything she set her mind on. Taha glanced at the sky and thanked the gods in utmost gratitude for sending Syun, who had uplifted her Soul.

Taha felt like a child again, as the water washed away years of misery. She knew this moment was rare and it would be up to her to cherish all that she had heard and learned today. Sometimes in life, we have moments so exhilarating that we feel completely alive and think that we are capable of living life to the fullest. But those moments of exhilaration fade in the mundaneness of life and they become memories that we often forget to hold on to.

Taha took one final dip into the waters and opened her eyes to see the clear and calm waters. As above, so below came to her mind, and she decided to never forget this episode in her life. She realised that change was inevitable. All one needed to do was embrace it, explore it and experiment with it.

As Taha stepped out of the lake, she glanced around and saw that Syun was nowhere to be seen. Suddenly, she broke out into a run and rushed towards the stone upon which he had been sitting. In the middle of the vast miles of nothingness, all that was left was a white feather on the stone.

Epilogue

The young man sat still like a statue and stared at the sky. It was a beautiful day, with the mist of rain hovering behind a sun-kissed sky. There were birds of prey flying high, dancing in rhythm with the wind. The ocean waves were creating a soothing rhythm, almost like a lover's call.

Young children were playing merrily while the older people watched, recalling their own childhood. The young man ate all of it and none of it. He was absorbed in his own mind. He did not notice the slender yet elegant young woman come up and sit beside him. She sat in a meditative pose with her eyes closed for a while.

When the time seemed right, she opened her eyes, looked at the young man and said, "Hi. I'm Taha. Want to hear a story?"

Acknowledgements

I would like to sincerely thank the entire team of Srishti Publishers and Distributors, my publishers, especially Arup Bose, and Alisha Verma Chopra, for their persistent efforts in making a dream come true. Additionally, I would also like to deeply thank Suhail Mathur, my literary agent, The Book Bakers, without whom none of this would have materialized.